# What's In Your Backpack?™

## ~ *Packing for Success in Life* ~

### Jimmy Cabrera, CSP

Publisher's Cataloging-in-Publication Data
*(Provided by Quality Books, Inc.)*

Cabrera, Jimmy.
    What's In Your Backpack? : packing for success in life./ Jimmy Cabrera.
        p. cm.
        Includes indes
        ISBN 1-893095-16-9

    1. Success.        I. Title.

BF637.S8C33 2002                    158.1
                                QBI02-200717


10   9   8   7   6   5   4   3

## Dedication <> Dedicación

With honor and humility I dedicate this book
to my wife, Laural. She is my strength, partner,
and inspiration. She has always been there
for me and by me. A pillar of encouragement,
she is always there to ensure that everyone she
comes in contact with will have a blessed day.
I also want to acknowledge three precious
gifts God gave me: my children -
Marcus, Alétta, and Chambray.

# Packing List

Believe Who You're Meant to Be • Live Life On Purpose •
Honor Your Heritage • Cultivate Your Special Talents • Give
Yourself Lip Service • Backpack Wisdom

Victim or Victor • Be Sure to Unpack • Hola 100 •
Backpack Wisdom

People Who Refused to Quit • Exaggerate the Positive •
Lighten Your Load • Never Lose Hope • The Fear Factor •
The Amazing Z Effect • Backpack Wisdom

Seek Profound Knowledge • Applied Knowledge is Power •
Nobody's Perfect • People Will Pay You For What You Know •
Lengthen Your Learning Curve • Make Wise Decisions •
Backpack Wisdom

# Preface

One of my favorite teachers used to say, "A short pencil is better than a long memory." Please read this book with a pencil (or pen or highlighter) in hand. Underline important points. Make notes to yourself in the margins or keep a notepad handy. Whenever you find a "keeper," highlight it or underline it so you won't lose it. My goal is to provide you with substantial content in this book so you can put meaningful insights and life-enriching tips in your backpack.

In the 17th Century, philosopher Benedict de Spinosa launched his own attitudinal "repacking." He realized that pursuing fame, wealth for wealth's sake and the pleasure of the senses would never make him completely happy. Fleeting things, he determined, lead to fleeting happiness and contentment. So, he gave us three cardinal rules to live by when it comes to creating the life you want:

- Comply with every general custom that does not hinder the nature and essence of your purpose.

- Indulge only in the pleasures that contribute to your health and well-being.

- Obtain sufficient monies and other aspects of wealth that are consistent with your overall life purpose and refrain from those that limit its expression.

Three hundred years or so later, the standards Spinosa set are still valid. Most of the success literature today pretty much offers the same advice:

- Figure out what your purpose is;
- Invest the time and energy in the right things; and
- Pack your backpack with the things that enable you to have purpose, and be prepared to unpack the things which slow your progress.

As I put the finishing touches on this book, I want to assure you that I have the utmost faith and confidence in your ability to become men and women of character. I believe you will want to make this world a better place for everyone. You are already well on your way toward making a difference, otherwise you would not have picked up this book.

# Introduction

As I write, we have turned the corner on a new millennium. Baby boomers have turned fifty, thirty-somethings are products of the Internet, and twenty-somethings are becoming entrepreneurs. We are still recovering from the shock and disbelief of the terrorists' attacks on the Pentagon and World Trade Center, and the fallout from many corporate debaucheries.

More and more of us are shifting our priorities and are searching for peace, harmony and spiritual balance. This has become even more important than our search for power, position, wealth and material things. This book is about redefining what success looks like in the new millennium, because we are living in an age of dichotomies. The ups and downs of the Stock Market mirror the rise and fall of corporations. People have lost their jobs, their retirement pensions and their trust in a system which has failed them.

The strength of this book stems from the fact that it gives you eight of the most powerful success tools you will ever find, regardless of how you define success. This book is for people who:

- keep themselves so busy that they lose sight of the most important things in life;
- read every article and book they see on wealth, financial security and getting ahead;
- want to have it all, spend it all and enjoy it all;
- want to simplify life and are taking steps toward it;
- love to cross things off their "to do" lists and count their achievements;
- dream big and stretch their limits at every turn;
- value peace and serenity, and understand the meaning of "going with the flow;"
- say they are happy, but feel an unsettling emptiness inside;
- have health challenges, but refuse to give in or give up;
- refuse to bury themselves in work by keeping work and play in perspective;
- have the courage to change and the will to succeed no matter what.

You know which of the above scenarios characterize your life. My guess is you picked this book up because you want more out of life. You want to be more successful at what you do and more adept at getting what you want. This probably isn't the first "how to succeed" book you've purchased, and I sincerely hope you will continue to value your personal and professional development.

If you bought this book to learn how to increase your income and build your net worth, you'll learn how to do that. If you bought it so you can improve important relationships and make them more satisfying, it can do that. If you selected this book because you believe it can help you understand yourself and improve your sense of direction, you are right again. If you think this book can help you find the balance and simplicity you seek, it'll definitely do that!

How can one book do all of that, you ask? How can one volume pack so many success principles into so few pages and still hit the mark? The secret of packing so much into so little came to me in a flash of insight. One morning I was sitting at the kitchen table next to my daughter's backpack. As I sat there pondering my research on success and happiness, it occurred to me that all of the research pointed to eight basic success factors. No matter how people defined success, my research revealed they had eight things in common. My dilemma that morning was how to package those eight success factors.

Another thoughtful glance at my daughter's backpack brought me to my feet. "That's it!" I exclaimed. "Our backpack will determine our success." I realized that morning that what we put in our "backpack of life" prepares us for our future and dictates our ultimate success. I quickly scribbled on my breakfast napkin the eight keys to success I had concluded from my research. To my surprise – and delight – I could match each success factor to one of the letters in the word B-A-C-K-P-A-C-K.

I realized that the backpack metaphor was perfect. All of us, whether we are adults or young people, stuff our backpacks with either positive or negative values, beliefs and attitudes. Most of us carry negative "tools" in our backpacks, which weight us down with heavy emotional loads. I looked at the eight success factors I had crayoned on the napkin. *"Eso es!"* I said to myself. That's Spanish for, "That's it!" What if we unpacked all of the negative, self-defeating emotional and attitudinal baggage, and repacked our backpacks with positive life-affirming principles?

As I stood there reveling in my discovery, the title of this book came to me: *What's in Your Backpack? Packing*

*For Success in Life.* I believe I'm able to pack so much life-changing content into so few pages because I have condensed all of the success research, to date, into eight major categories. All successful people use these golden principles in one form or another:

$B$elieve in yourself

$A$ttitude is everything

$C$ourage to stretch your limits

$K$nowledge sought and applied

$P$eople skills ensure your success

$A$lways set realistic goals

$C$ommit to excellence in everything you do

$K$eep dreaming big

This success formula will work if you work. If you've been trudging down the school of hard knocks, the principles outlined in this book will turn you into a *road scholar*. If you've run into too many blind alleys, it will help you see a better way. If you're tired of wandering, dragging and walking tediously up hill, it will help you hit the trail running. You'll be able to turn the stones on your path into golden opportunities of success. Millions of people have done it, and so can you.

# Believe in Yourself

# Chapter 1

# Believe in Yourself

*Look, I really don't want to wax philosophic, but I will say that if you're alive, you've got to flap your arms and legs, you've got to jump around a lot, you've got to make a lot of noise...As I see it, if you're quiet, you're not living. You've got to be noisy, or at least your thoughts should be noisy and colorful and lively.* (Mel Brooks)

Believing in yourself is singularly the most important thing you can do to guarantee your success in life. When you believe in yourself and in your talents, abilities and worthiness, you are able to make better choices. And when you make better choices, you are able to improve your life. Believing in yourself allows you to act purposefully and boldly; to have faith in your ideas, talents and abilities; to know on a deeper level that you will do what is right for yourself and others.

We are all born with an innate sense of our uniqueness, our own distinct individuality. We know there is more to us than meets the eye. There is a feeling of sureness in our bones that we are put here for a purpose. This purpose is the essence of our life, that special "something" which determines our destiny. We all enter the world with a purpose. Our special calling cannot be postponed, avoided or dismissed. It can possess us completely. We are all subject to the push of our individuality. And we are all subject to the pull of procrastination. George Allen shares a great insight on the nature of procrastination using the following example:

Every morning in Africa
a Gazelle wakes up. It knows
it must run faster than the
fastest Lion or it will be killed.

Every morning a Lion wakes up.
It knows it must often outrun the
slowest Gazelle or it will starve to death.

So, it does not matter whether you
are a Lion or a Gazelle, for when the
sun comes up you had better be running.

Our challenge does not lie in finishing the task. It lies in the simplicity of getting started. It means getting up every morning and running toward our success as fast as our eduction, knowledge and skills can take us. Please remember that procrastination usually results in regrets, guilt and stagnation. Let me teach you a new word in Spanish/English, referred to as *Spanglish*. The *Spanglish* word for procrastination is *Procrastamañana*.

7

> *Our challenge does not lie in finishing the task. It lies in the simplicity of getting started.*

When we make the decision to start believing in ourselves and going forward to reach our next level of success, certain situations will pop up and test our enthusiasm. I am sure you recognize the negative effects of procrastination. I call procrastination the "tomorrow syndrome," the "I'll wait until I gather all the facts syndrome" or "the time is not quite right to proceed syndrome."

**A Backpack Keeper:** Procrastination is the brakes your lack of confidence uses to stall your future.

## Be Who You're Meant to Be

The challenge for each of us is to discover the path that is uniquely our own and have faith so we can follow it to achieve our individual dreams. Each step you take toward believing in yourself brings you that much closer to fulfilling your life's mission.

This means knowing who you are and who you aren't. Expressing your true nature is critical to your success because it is the only thing which authenticates your journey and keeps your life on track. Without it, you are

8

rudderless, cast adrift on the sea of life, carried by currents of frustration and doubt.

The driving force behind the discovery of your life purpose is discovering who you are and why you are. You determine what legacy you want to leave behind, what contributions you are capable of making and what your life narrative is all about. Your life purpose is your self-definition. Your specialness, your uniqueness, is the ultimate statement of who you are. It is the inner compass that guides you to express your uniqueness.

How each of us comes to feel about our individuality, our specialness, has a strong influence on how we feel about the uniqueness in others. It affects whether we grow into mature adults who rejoice in a world filled with diversity or into biased adults who fear, and even resent, diversity.

One of the important life tasks is the discovery of and appreciation for our uniqueness. One of my roles as a professional speaker is to help people of all socio-economic levels and ethnicities realize how rare and valuable they are – that each of us has something no one else has: our own individual, God-given purpose.

One of the questions of life that we have to face is: What will be our life story? I like to refer to life as *from womb-to-tomb*. When we are born, we are given a birth certificate, and when we die, we are issued a death certificate. There is a start and then there is a finish. It all comes down to what we put in between. Time is all we have, so let's not waste it. I want to make a request and at the same time deliver a challenge. I want you to get out of your comfort zone. Visualize a small one-gallon fish bowl that has one small goldfish. Many people are like this goldfish. They are very content with smallness. However, to become what we are meant to be, we must see the world outside the fish bowl. We must see that there is so much out there waiting for us to experience, and make our claim. So, I encourage you to turn your goldfish thinking into a whale perspective and unleash your unlimited potential.

> **When your heart is in the right place, your feet will usually follow.**

Too often we undervalue our talents and question our worth. We hesitate to accept new challenges because we are unsure of ourselves. It is important to remember that behind all of the reasons we give for not believing in ourselves is our failure to listen to ourselves.

All of the justifications we use for not believing in ourselves are just shallow excuses to hang on to our self-doubts, fears and lack of confidence. When we give ourselves permission to discover who we really are, we open up possibilities that are meant for us.

**A Backpack Keeper:** No one behaves exactly like you. I'll bet even you have trouble being yourself sometimes.

# Live Life On Purpose

Believing in yourself is believing in your purpose. It means believing that your being here means something – that you have value and worth. Brian Tracy puts it wonderfully when he says: "There are no extra human beings; you are here on this earth to do something special with your life." People who live life on purpose believe in themselves and in their ability to stay M.A.D. (**M**ake **A D**ifference). Those who believe they have the power to shape the basic answers of their lives see themselves as especially M.A.D.D. (**M**ake **A D**eliberate **D**ifference). I've used the four-character abbreviation of M.A.D.D. (Mothers Against Drunk Driving), the organization founded by Candy Lightner, to define living life on purpose. It is this deliberateness to make a difference that turns wishful thinking into life purpose. People *on purpose* "wear out" instead of "rust out."

Living life on purpose usually involves changing lifestyle and workstyle habits in order to bring them into alignment with our true nature. Believing in this singleness of purpose helps us gain a sense of clarity. Once we know who we are, we begin to eliminate emotional, mental, physical and material handcuffs. There is an old, amusing story you may be familiar with -- I personally love the story -- that helps illustrate the importance of taking off the handcuffs:

> *Once upon a time, two frogs fell into a bucket filled with cream. Realizing their plight, both frogs began thrashing about in the ocean of cream in an effort to swim closer to the rim of the basket. One frog, seeing that there was no way to get a firm footing in the warm liquid, complained and threatened to stop swimming.*
>
> *The second frog encouraged him not to give up, and noted that the liquid appeared to be thickening unexplainably. The first frog took his observation to heart and replied that what was once easy going was now becoming too much like work. The second frog believed that the hard work*

*would eventually pay off, but his amphibian col-
league accepted his fate and drowned.*

*Deciding he'd rather wear himself out than
admit defeat, the remaining frog thrashed even
harder to stay afloat. He repeated aloud to himself
"I think I can. I think I can." (Sound like another
familiar story?) Okay. Where were we? Oh, yes,
after a while, his persistence paid off. His faithful
churning had turned the cream into butter.*

*With his new vantage point atop the butter, he
paused long enough to appreciate his hard work
and to snag a few flies which were attracted by the
newly-made butter. Then, with a leap that would
have made an Olympic athlete proud, he hopped
off the bucket of doom.*

Oftentimes our true nature rises from the depths of our
subconscious to the top of our character when we are faced
with adversity. We can keep our authentic self buried or
express our true nature and abilities. All we have to do is
believe in ourselves and believe we have a greater purpose
beyond ourselves. By the way, the word "believe" comes
from the two English words, "by" and "live," meaning to
"live by something." Therefore, discover and identify your
"something" and live by it, so your best will come out.

Much of my speaking career involves helping people
and organizations accomplish success through excellence. I
believe in that philosophy so strongly that I named my
speaking business *Success Through Excellence*. I've made a
practice of interviewing people in my audiences who have
achieved excellence in their fields of expertise through their
skills, education, attitudes and experience. Although my
interviews were not intended to be a rigorous scientific
study, I can report that in every case there were two common success factors among these highly-productive and

happy people: they believed in themselves and they had a clear sense of purpose.

From a theological view, each one of these people saw himself or herself as a steward of his or her life purpose. They believed they were responsible for contributing to something enduring and worthwhile. More than anything else, they understood who they were.

The more I study personal development and human behavior, the more I strengthen my conclusion on values and character. By the time we are seven years of age, 70% of all our values and character are in place and in our backpacks. When we hit the ripe old age of 18 to 20, 97% of our values and character are in place and in our backpacks. Then we spend the rest of our lives fine-tuning the remaining 3% of our values and character.

> **A Backpack Keeper:** Our ultimate life-enriching job is not to blame ourselves for our past mistakes, but to fix our course for the future.

# Honor Your Heritage

Honoring our ancestral roots helps connect us with the historical us, but it also helps define who we are today and what we can be tomorrow. Our lineage is the basis for our individuality and our perspective on life. It is the ground metaphor for everything we think, feel and do. It is that special ethnic version of us that is unique and unreplicable.

However, I didn't always feel this way. I'd like to give you a snapshot of my youth that illustrates the special perspectives we get from our heritage that leave life-long impressions.

I hope no one reading this book suffered from low self-esteem as I did when I was young. As a matter of fact, I didn't like myself much. I believed the only way I could become successful was for my skin to be white. Please allow me to share my story so you can see where I am headed with the lessons you will learn from this book.

I was reared in two small communities in the panhandle of Northern Texas. I was born in Amherst and lived there until I was nine before we moved to Muleshoe. The heritage of my family is of Mexican descent. My three brothers and I were the first Latinos who were allowed to attend the public school, even though the schools were not integrated. I recall vividly the discrimination we experienced. I am sure you are familiar with the adage, "Sticks and stones may break my bones, but words will never hurt me." Well, I want you to know that's not true. Words do hurt, and they can have a negative impact on a human being. The scars they leave can last a lifetime. Can anyone else besides me relate to that?

I remember the names some of the kids called me. For instance, I was called *messcon* (note what the first four letters spell: *mess*), as if to imply that my culture was a messed up race. I also heard words like: *Pancho, wet-back, greaser* and *spic*. But the one I hated the most was *Tamale Joe*. I had one teacher who, when he called roll, would call me Jose. To him all Latino males were Jose and Latinas were Rosie. I would correct him and tell him my name was Jimmy and not Jose, but he refused to correct himself. To make matters worse, the class followed his lead.

We lived eight or nine blocks from school, and because of the way I was treated at times, I would catch myself crying on the way to and from school. I couldn't understand why I was treated so differently from my classmates. After

14

school hours, I had some classmates who would not hang out with me because their parents would not let them associate with Mexican kids.

In some of the cafes in the surrounding areas, you could see signs in the windows: *Whites Only*. Can you believe that in some Texas communities signs were placed in store windows or front yards that read, *No Dogs or Blacks Allowed*? I learned later they were referring to Mexicans as dogs. I didn't want to be a Chihuahua. I just wanted to be Jimmy!

Since my parents couldn't afford meal tickets at school, my mother made my lunch. She would make *tacos con papa y huevo* (that is a flour tortilla with potato and egg). And man, were they good. At lunch period no one would sit next to me, so I would find myself a corner to eat my lunch.

One day, a classmate asked me. "Hey, whacha eating?"

Intimidated and embarrassed I said nothing. To my surprise he sat next to me and took out his lunch. He pulled out a square-looking meal. Instead of telling him what I was eating, I asked him what he was eating.

He said, "This is a bologna sandwich."

Up to that point in my life, I had never seen a bologna sandwich. So I questioned him.

"What's a bologna sandwich?"

He was shocked and said: "What, are you stupid?" Then he sarcastically asked, "What's that thing you're eating?"

I said, "Well, I am eating a *taco con papa y huevo.*"

He said, "What's that?"

I smiled and said, "And you call me stupid?"

We laughed and exchanged our lunches.

The next few days we continued trading our lunches. Then his buddies wanted to trade their lunches. Their interest gave me an idea. I asked mom to make me six or eight tacos for lunch because I was very hungry. Now don't get ahead of me. If you guessed that I started selling them, you are correct. I had my own little taco stand. I sold them for ten cents each. Not bad, wouldn't you agree? I could buy a 6-ounce cola, bag of chips and a piece of gum for ten cents. I had a thriving business until mom found out and I had to close shop.

An experience I had at a local retail store changed my life altogether. My mom took me shopping for a pair of jeans. As we entered the small store, we were approached by a salesperson who asked what we were doing in the store since Mexicans weren't allowed to shop there. My mother's English skills were not that good at the time, so I had to explain to her in Spanish why we couldn't shop there.

My mom was a very proud and tall woman...about 5'2"...well, she was tall to me! To her credit, she didn't cause a scene. She said, "Okay, let's leave. But we will walk out of here with our heads held high and with pride." She headed toward the front door thinking I was beside her. When she noticed I wasn't at her side, she retraced her steps and found me sitting in one of the aisles. I was embarrassed and crying.

"*Mi higo, levanta la cara,*" (Son, lift your face) she said softly, "because we will be walking out of here with pride and with our heads held high."

I didn't budge.

She repeated herself twice before she took more drastic action. My mother could really pinch – how about your mother? She pinched me under my arm and escorted me from the store. I must tell you about my mom's pinching expertise. When she pinched you on the outside of your arm, it was bad enough. But if she pinched you on the inside of your arm, it was very painful. I walked obediently – and quickly – on my tip-toes out of the store with her vice-like pinching hold prompting my every step.

She pinched me all the way home, lecturing me about being prideful, never being ashamed, to always believe in myself, and to always walk with my head high. I want you to know that ever since that day, I have never lowered my head in any circumstance. It doesn't matter how anyone criticizes me or rejects me. I choose to hold my head high. It's a good choice, wouldn't you agree? If I see a young person walking all slumped with his or her head down, I have been known to get their attention. I will say to them, "What are you looking for, a bunch of pennies?" Then I encourage them to walk upright and hold their head high.

I cannot tell you the number of individuals who find it difficult to accept who they are, their heritage, culture, family and where they live. Another thing that disturbs me is that although we are living in the United States, which is a great melting pot of all cultures, there are individuals who refuse to accept the culture of their neighbors.

In 1915, my grandfather on my dad's side packed up his belongings and, with his wife and two sons, headed north to the United States of America. He had heard of the place that was labeled the "land of opportunity" and he wanted to provide a better life for his family. They traveled by chuck wagon from Jalisco, Mexico to Texas. The trip was over 700 miles. Finally they settled in Wharton County, which is 75 miles southeast of Houston. At the time, my dad was about two years old.

In 1939, Dad decided it was time for him to seek better opportunities for his family. His brother had left Texas and migrated to central California. He wrote to my dad and asked him to consider moving to California. So Dad packed up his belongings and, with his wife and one-year old son, headed for California. He left El Campo, Texas in a 1936 Ford, with $100 in his pocket. He traveled north through Texas and ran out of money in a little community called Amherst. In spite of all the things my family went through, running out of money and settling there was the best thing that ever happened to Dad. He became the first janitor for the county hospital and then later started his own janitorial business.

Have you noticed that when refugees come to this great land, they seem to be more successful than the average native-born American? Have you ever wondered why? I believe that it is because the refugee is good to the opportunity and many native-born Americans wait for an opportunity to be good to them.

> *Don't wait for an opportunity to be good to you; be good to the opportunity.*

This is the photograph of the house that we lived in when I was a boy.

I was the youngest of a family of seven (including my grandmother) who lived in this 200-square foot house. We lived there until I was five years old. It was a wood frame type building with two small rooms – a bedroom and a living area that included a kitchen area. It had no inside plumbing. In my presentations over the last 19 years, I have shown this photo, via slide, to over one million people. I do not show the house to draw any sympathy from the audience. I show it to remind people to *never be ashamed of who you are, where you live, your family or anything.* I sometimes say it in Spanish and then repeat it in English to make the point. Spanish: *Nunca tenga pena de su herencia, donde viven, su familia o de nada.*

I can't mention culture and heritage without mentioning September 11, 2001. Not long ago, I was looking at some pictures of the World Trade Center. One of the photos that caught my attention was the one that showed what remained of the buildings I still look at the photo and lift up the families in prayer. People refer to the area as Ground Zero. Well, I believe it should be referred to as Ground Hero. To my understanding, approximately 3,100 people lost their lives that day. They represented over 80 different cultures and heritages. But only one color of blood flowed that day and it was red. Are we really that different from each other? In my opinion, our commonalities far exceed our differences.

I can't give a speech without telling my audiences how proud I am of being an American. That same sentiment applies in writing this book. I love this land and if you were to cut my finger I would bleed red, white, and blue. Yes, I am a flag-waving fool. I realize that America is not perfect, but I assure you that America is an awesome country.

During one of my presentations, I made the statement that I was proud to be an American. From the back of the large room filled with over 1,500 attendees someone yelled: "I hate America." That statement hit a nerve, and without thinking I responded by saying, "Really? Then come on down and show your face. I'll buy you a one-way ticket to Iraq." I meant no disrespect to Iraq. But I would buy that person a one-way ticket to any third-world country with the understanding that they can never set foot on American soil again. I guarantee you that person would undoubtedly change his or her attitude about our great land.

When I include the above segment on America in my speeches, I ask my audiences to spell the word *American*. Then I ask them to repeat the last four letters: I CAN. So as an American you can always say, I Can. Pretty cool, don't you agree? Well, I guess I am a lucky person because God made me a MexICAN. I get to say I Can twice. I am a Mex-ICAN-AmerICAN. AfrICAN-AmerICANs get to say it twice, too. So you see, we can all have the "I can" attitude.

> ***"Success comes in cans, not cannots."***
> ***(Joel Weldon)***

I gave a presentation in a high school with 3,000 students in the gym. At the end of the program a student came up to me and said, "Mr. Jimmy, I am proud of myself, because, you see, my mother is Mexican and my dad is Black. I guess that makes me 'Blaxican.'" We both grinned. His statement had quite an impact on me, because I realized something I said made him proud of his heritage.

Our genes are the biological part of our life narrative. And while they don't tell our whole story, they are part of what makes us who we are. Understanding our ancestral roots and our genealogical past is absolutely necessary for helping us find our rightful place in our future. Believing in our future worth comes from believing in our ancestral worth. "Our legacy," said Oliver Wendell Holmes, "is an omnibus in which all our ancestors ride." Honoring those common threads allows us to knit the fabric of our future self into a tapestry of beauty and individuality.

In a very real sense, our heritage is our ancestral compass. It is the genealogical foundation of our core being. I believe we can never fully understand the complexity or the innate richness of our lives without comprehending the context of our beginnings. Family histories should be preserved and handed down as legacies to succeeding generations.

*AmerICAN*

*MexICAN*

*AfrICAN*

We are all heirs of our heritages. I am certainly proud of my Mexican-American heritage. I believe part of my birthright as an American citizen is to honor and express the Mexican-American part of me. Ralph Waldo Emerson put it this way: "Each one of us finds room in a few square inches on our face for the traits of our ancestors and for the expression of all our history." My attitudes, beliefs, values and physical characteristics are updates of my family's genealogical "album."

**A Backpack Keeper:** Our ancestry is that special ethnic version of us that makes us unique and unreplicable.

# Cultivate Your Special Talents

Everyone has some kind of talent. Accepting ourselves for who we are and for the talents and abilities we are given is part of our fundamental calling. Accepting ourselves, warts and all, is a precondition for discovering, and then developing, the talents we have. Some of us are beautiful, tall, lean and athletic. Others are comely, short, a little over-weight, but fairly athletic. Most of us have some kind of pimple or freckle, wart or mole, birthmark or blemish. Some of us are the picture of health while others have health challenges or life-threatening health problems. Everyone I know or have met has faults, shortcomings and Achilles' heels.

Despite our imperfections, we have talents and abilities that compensate for our spots, specks, creases and wrinkles. As I mentioned earlier in this chapter, as a youngster I had difficulty accepting who I was. I thought it was a liability until the love of my mother and the insight of a sculptor turned what I saw as a liability into an asset.

Michelangelo carved *David* from a flawed block of marble. Another sculptor had begun work on the huge block of marble and then abandoned it when he discovered a flaw. The deep gash in the side of the block made the stone "unworthy," and therefore useless to many talented sculptors for decades. Michelangelo, however, saw something in the marble worth revealing – a special quality no one else saw. He accepted the marble, imperfections and all, and created a masterpiece.

His willingness to accept a piece of marble the way it was and turn it into a masterpiece helped me realize that my Mexican-American heritage is an asset, not a liability. It is a monument to my individuality. And because God is my sculptor, He has taken what I thought in my youth to be a birth defect and turned my heritage into a one-of-a-kind masterpiece called Jimmy Cabrera. Of course, God is not through with me yet, but I accept who I am and believe I am put here for a very special purpose.

I have found in my own life that it is important to believe in my own special talents and abilities, develop them further and use them to help others. People tell me I am a strong catalyst, motivator and speaker. I take pride in helping people discover their own talents and abilities. It brings me great joy to see people discover their own richness and uniqueness. I may not be the most talented speaker or author on the planet, but I work hard at it. Like Erma Bombeck, "When I stand before God at the end of my life, I hope I won't have a single bit of talent left and will say, 'God, I used everything you gave me.'"

> **Give yourself permission to win.**

Do you have a talent for finding the best fishing holes or lost animals? Do you have a knack for numbers, managing details, or remembering birthdays and anniversaries? Do you have an eye for color, an ear for music, a taste for fine wine, or a touch that heals? Can you play the piano, sing in the choir, or direct a music team? Are you clever with finances, a whiz on the computer, or a pro on the Internet? Can you hit a tee shot three hundred yards down the fairway, kick a soccer ball the length of the field, or dance the salsa with grace and elegance? Can you speak to youth on their level, draw a "straight line," or hear the nuances in someone's cry for help? Can you speak several languages, prepare a gourmet meal, or take extraordinary photographs?

Talented people are talented because they work at it. Dan Millman said in his book, *No Ordinary Moments*, that "successful professionals in the fields of athletics, acting, law, medicine and business attribute their success more to hard work than to natural talent."

If we are not careful, we can be very hard on ourselves. You may be familiar with the phrase, "We have found the enemy and it is us." Ray Pelletier, a speaker friend of mine, gave me a great phrase and I want you to know it, embrace it, master it and commit to it. It can change your life. The phrase is: *Give yourself permission to win.* It's okay to believe in yourself, to excel, to build strong self-esteem and expect more out of life. Another friend of mine, Jim Jacobus, uses a great phrase: *Living life large.* Isn't that a powerful life-affirming statement?

People like Jesse Owens take *giving yourself permission to win* to its next level. Jesse, as most of you know, was a great American athlete, and to me a great, positive role model. In high school my favorite sport was track and field. One day I was reading about the challenges Jesse faced as a person of color. All of his accomplishments inspired me to put my heart into the sport. Although I never had the privilege of meeting him, I learned his formula for success:

> *Passion leads to desire, desire leads to work, and work leads to success.*

He taught me that passion without purpose is wishful thinking. With a clearly defined purpose, your passion will lead you toward work that is right for you. For example, in my profession I have a passion to speak, to help others realize their unique potential. Every time I speak, I try to *make a difference* in the lives of the people attending my presentations. I take my job seriously. I am very aware of the tremendous responsibility I have when I step up to the podium. I've brought that same passion to this book, because I want you to be a highly successful *backpack* person.

I believe that raw talent, coupled with a good attitude and hard work, creates an unstoppable combination. I also believe that when you consistently use and refine your innate talents and abilities, you will meet with a success beyond your wildest dreams.

> **A Backpack Keeper:**
> Today's accomplishments were
> yesterday's potential.

# Give Yourself Lip Service

Using positive self-talk is critical to your success. I am not referring to arrogance, pounding on your chest as if you were Tarzan, but a simple approach to self-talk. Regardless of how you define success, what you say leaves a powerful impression on your consciousness. If repeated often enough, certain words and key phrases can literally change your entire outlook on life. I'm not kidding! I'm going to paraphrase what I just said. Your self-talk can *literally* determine how successful or unsuccessful you will be in life. Still think it's too strong a statement? I'm going to share some extraordinary research with you that revolutionized the way we understood ourselves over 30 years ago. The studies have been replicated many times and have proven to be quite accurate and reliable.

A landmark study was conducted at the University of Pennsylvania by physicist David Bohm, who proved that any thought which is repeated strongly enough, with emotional weight and a sense of absoluteness, leaves grooves in our gray matter. This is now he describes the process:

> *When experiments have been done with radioactive tracers to see what happens inside the brain, every idea, every feeling creates a radical redistribution of the blood in the brain. If you keep bringing blood into a certain pattern all the time, you begin to grow more cells there, and less cells somewhere else. With very strong thoughts, the synapses get very fixed, creating grooves in the brain's neuro pathways.*

It doesn't take a rocket scientist (in this case a physicist) to realize that if the very physiology of the human brain is affected by our long-held thoughts and feelings AND if the synapses really do get fixed, then we have the power to program *grooves of success* in our brain. According to researchers who specialize in bio-feedback and brain lateralization research, most of the repetitive negative feelings, thoughts and attitudes we have about ourselves are stored in our right hemisphere (our verbal side) along with our positive thoughts and attitudes.

> **As a man thinketh in his heart,**
> **so shall he be.**

Inventory your self-talk. Do you say self-deprecating things like: "Boy, was I stupid," or "What a klutz I am," or "If I had half a brain…"? If you use derogatory words like these to describe yourself, it's time to reprogram your messages and turn negative grooves into positive ones. Use positive self-talk statements like:

- I make wise choices every day.
- I believe in myself and make a positive difference in people's lives.

> **Self-talk contributes to your "Believe-Ability."**

One of my favorite self-talk statements is one I learned 25 years ago from the founder of the National Speakers Association, Cavett Robert. Please etch these ten two-letter words in your mind, and in your backpack, because they are powerful words: "If it is to be, it is up to me." In Spanish, it's only seven words: *Si tiene que ser, depende de mi.* But the meaning is the same in any language: *S'il doit être, il est jusqu'à moi* (French); *Wenn es sein soll, ist es bis zu mir* (German); *Se deve essere, spetta me* (Italian); *Se dever ser, é até mim* (Portuguese); *Als het moet zijn, is het tot me* (Dutch).

As you know, I love to present in schools and one day I spoke to 800 first graders. We were in a large room with no chairs and the kids all sat on the floor for the program. They got pretty loud. You have no clue what 150 decibels sounds like until you're surrounded by 800 first graders. A bit concerned, I spoke with the principal and asked if the students could tone down and give me their attention.

The principal said, "Sure, Jimmy, no problem. I'll just give the quiet sign."

She proceeded to give the quiet sign and to my amazement, within a few seconds the group came to order and you could hear a pin drop. I was impressed. *This lady is good*, I said to myself.

I told the students that they would need to remember ten words. *If it is to be – it is up to me*. I divided the room in half. One half of the room, on my command, would say the first five words, *if it is to be;* and the other half would say the last five words, *it is up to me*. We had Teams A and B ready to roll in a competitive spirit. We made some noise that day.

Then I explained the importance of the last five words: *it is up to me*. I asked them as a group to finish each sentence that I'd started. They were to repeat "it is up to me" every time I raised my hand. I said a few things like:

| Jimmy | 800 plus students/teachers |
| --- | --- |
| Do my own work | It is up to me |
| Pay attention in class | It is up to me |
| Help my teacher | It is up to me |
| Respect everybody | It is up to me |
| Never cheat | It is up to me |
| Never lie | It is up to me |
| Never smoke cigarettes | It is up to me |
| Never drink alcohol | It is up to me |
| Never use drugs | It is up to me |
| Help mom and dad at home | It is up to me |

I did this exercise for over five minutes. Can you imagine the energy we generated in that room? Would you say that what we did was impressive? Well, let me tell you what impressed *me*. After the short assembly, the kids were dismissed and I observed them as they left the room. Looking down the hall, I overheard many of the students saying, "If it is to be – it is up to me." I stood there, enjoying the moment. Where would you and I be now if we had believed in the meaning of *if it is to be – it is up to me* when we were five years old? It doesn't matter whether your age is 6 or 106, these powerful words will make a difference in your life and career.

**IF IT IS TO BE – IT IS UP TO ME!**

Call me corny, but these powerful words have helped me build my speaking business. I say them enthusiastically every day. My wife, Laural, and my children use them. I have them posted in my office. They are indelibly written on my heart. They contribute to my "believe-ability" in my talents, education and skills.

I am constantly striving to improve my "believe-ability." Like any other kind of ability, it takes time to develop a nurturing environment and commitment. I make it a daily practice to say positive things to myself about myself. When it comes to believing in yourself and recognizing your own self-worth, it's okay to say good things about yourself. I'm not saying that egotistically. I'm simply suggesting that you define yourself in more positive, complimentary terms instead of negative, self-denigrating terms.

Read the following list of words as if they applied to you:

| | |
|---|---|
| abusive | egotistical |
| belligerent | foolish |
| cowardly | gluttonous |
| devious | harsh |

How did they make you feel? Chances are, if they really were words you used to describe yourself, you wouldn't be feeling good about yourself at this point. If these were words people used to describe you, or they were words you habitually used to describe yourself, your self-image would be taking quite a hit. On the other hand, words like the following list of adjectives are more likely to bring a smile to your face and heighten your self-concept if they were used to describe you. Read them now, as if they applied to you, and see how you feel:

| | |
|---|---|
| athletic | enterprising |
| brilliant | fantastic |
| clever | doer |
| positive | successful |

You're still smiling, aren't you? Because these are powerful, self-affirming words, their positive impact on your consciousness affects every cell in your body. They leave positive grooves in your brain and translate into positive thoughts and attitudes.

**A Backpack Keeper:** The words you use to describe yourself today help dictate who you will be tomorrow.

# Backpack Wisdom

1. Belief in yourself is singularly the most important thing you can add to your backpack to be successful in life.

2. When you give yourself permission to connect with your true nature, you open up the possibilities that were meant for your successful journey through life.

3. People who live life on purpose believe in themselves and in their ability to stay M.A.D. (Make A Difference)

4. Your heritage is the genealogical foundation of your core being, it's your ancestral compass, your genetic pedigree, the thread that holds your backpack together.

5. Raw talent, a good attitude and hard work are an unstoppable combination.

6. Be careful what words you use to describe yourself. Only use positive words and phrases.

B

**A**ttitude Is Everything

C

K

P

A

C

K

# Chapter 2

## Attitude Is Everything

*Any fact facing us is not as important as our attitude toward it, for that determines our success or failure.* (Norman Vincent Peale)

Attitude is everything. That simple expression has so much meaning attached to it that entire books have been written on the subject. I have included it as one of the key items in your backpack because it underwrites the other eight success factors. Maintaining a positive, "can-do" attitude is central to your success in all areas of your life. I believe you can't have a successful journey through life without a positive mental attitude.

The average person has over 64,000 thoughts each day. If my math is right, that would mean a little over 2,666 thoughts every hour and 44 separate and distinct thoughts every minute. That's a lot of thought power. Most people's thoughts are a hodgepodge of internal inclinations about money, work, meals, homework, rent or mortgage payments, child rearing, grocery shopping, what TV show to record on the VCR, which lane to merge quickly into on the way home from work or school, and so on.

Keeping track of all of those thoughts is not something most people do on a daily basis. People don't have any idea of the kind of thoughts they have – whether they're positive or negative, fleeting or introspective, assumptions or facts, self-enriching or self-nullifying. Most people have no real appreciation for the amount of internal dialogue that hums incessantly through their brains. The $64,000 question is how many of those 64,000 thoughts are negative vs. positive, self-enriching vs. self-nullifying?

Unfortunately, most of our mental chatter *is* negative. We are bombarded with negative messages like: "Don't do this," or "Don't do that," or "Don't rock the boat," or "You'll never amount to anything," or "That will never work here."

Negative perspectives do serve an important function when it comes to certain kinds of advice, counseling and caution when clarity and direction are needed. However, when negation dominates the thinking process itself, it becomes an unhealthy internal censor. I call habitual negative thinking *Backpack Overload*. Just like a backpack that is overloaded can actually cause you physical pain, the negative thoughts of your mind can cause you emotional pain.

I am a simple person who doesn't usually ask for much. As a customer entering any place of business I expect, or should I say hope, I will receive good customer service. It doesn't take much to make me happy when it comes to being a customer or guest in any service establishment. However, I'd like to tell you about an experience I had that illustrates how *Backpack Overload* on the part of a convenience store clerk lost an important customer.

One day I had an appointment with a client and headed toward the other side of Houston. On my way I noticed that the fuel gauge on my car showed empty. So I stopped at my favorite convenience store to gas up. I paid for the gas at the pump, then decided I wanted to get a snack. When I went inside, I noticed that the clerk at the counter was treating customers rudely. I picked up a soft drink and a small package of crackers and headed to the counter. While I was waiting for my turn to pay, I started to psyche myself up to face this negative employee.

I thought to myself, *don't let this person's negative attitude affect you. Remember you are a motivational speaker, and when you get up to the counter it is your job to change her attitude.*

As I made it up to the front of the line I said, "Good morning, my name is Jimmy Cabrera and I'm a motivational speaker. I couldn't help noticing that you have been very negative to the customers. So I was wondering what I could say to help change your negative attitude."

The clerk never looked up, totally ignoring me. I placed my soft drink and the package of crackers on the counter. The clerk grabbed my soft drink and tried to scan it. The scanner would not register, so she tapped the bottle until finally she heard the beep. Then she grabbed the package of crackers and the same thing happened, but this time she used more force. Originally my package of crackers contained six small peanut butter crackers. When she was done, the package was reduced to twenty cracker bits. The clerk spoke to me without looking up, mumbling "That will be $1.97." Reluctantly I handed her $2.00. I placed my hand out with my palm up waiting for my change. Still without making eye contact, she dropped my change on the counter, deliberately missing my open palm.

Normally, when my change is in pennies, I drop them into the penny jar next to the register. I was so irritated that I picked up my change and headed out. As I approached the exit, it occurred to me that I was a regular customer. Although I had not seen this particular clerk before, I felt she had no reason to treat me – or anyone else – this way.

I did an about face and went back to the counter. I excused myself to the customer at the counter and addressed the clerk. "Excuse me, I have unfinished business here. Miss. MISS!" I continued, "I have been a customer here for over ten years and if you ever want me to return, you had best say thank you to me!" The clerk finally gave me eye-contact and said, "It's on the receipt."

I looked and sure enough, *thank you* was imprinted on the receipt. At that moment, I fired that convenience store and have never gone back. I guess the clerk did not realize that *Attitude Is Everything*.

The more I mature in my profession, the more I am convinced that attitude makes all the difference in an individual's success. We have all heard the phrases, *check your attitude, change your attitude* and *your attitude stinks*. Have you ever stopped to think what the meaning is behind these statements? Webster defines attitude as a manner of feeling, mood or thinking that shows one's disposition, opinion and mental state. We can have positive attitudes or negative ones, like the clerk at the convenience store.

This chapter focuses on the other half of the thinking process – the positive side that says: a positive attitude is everything! As William James, the great American philosopher and psychologist said, "The greatest discovery of my generation is that human beings can alter their lives by altering their attitudes, and they can alter their attitudes by altering their thinking."

> **A Backpack Keeper:** Attitude is your inward thinking that becomes your outward thinking and behavior.

# Victim or Victor

Sometimes bad things happen to good people. Some people are victims of domestic violence, prejudice, automobile accidents, child abuse or neglect, war and unfortunately, terrorist bombings. People who go through those types of horrible experiences clearly qualify as victims. Other people are victimized by the horrific power and devastation caused by hurricanes, tornadoes, earthquakes, floods, fires and volcanic eruptions. More and more people suffer from diseases such as cancer, heart attacks, diabetes, multiple sclerosis, Parkinson's and leukemia.

The odds are that all of us will be faced with a natural disaster or a serious accident or illness at some time in our lives. But more than anything else, I believe it's the choices we make and the attitudes that spawn them, not the circumstances we face, that determine our future happiness, prosperity and success. Some people are into *victimology*. I call it the PLOM disease, the **P**oor **L**ittle **O**ld **M**e outlook on life. You've heard people with the PLOM disease, haven't you? They say things like:

"I'm not smart enough to be class president."
"I'll never make enough money to buy a nice car
like that."
"Other people always get all the breaks."
"I'm the most unlucky person in the world."

These people shirk their responsibility and blame their misfortunes and lost opportunities on other people. They use their wounds as a badge of honor. Their problems and disappointments are effective ways of getting attention they might not otherwise receive.

The attention they get is not the attention they need, of course, but it keeps other people from providing "real" support. PLOM disease is an attitude *dis-ease*. It is much easier to live with the *dis-ease*, secretly longing for self-respect, but publicly complaining out loud to gain sympathy for self-imposed limitations.

```
STOP...CRYING...START...TRYING

STOP...CRYING...START...STUDYING

STOP...CRYING...START...PRAYING
```

As I mentioned earlier, esteem is believing in yourself and in your future. You can build your life on negatives or positives. I hope you'll choose to build your life on the positives, because there are enough negatives in this world. You don't need to add any more negatives to your backpack. For example, let me show you how easy it is to build a negative belief system. Look at the word B.U.I.L.D.

**B**elieving falsehoods like: there is no future, no one cares, using negative self-talk, etc.

**U**ncertain attitude: fearing the future.

**I** can't attitude: sense there's no possibility, I am good for nothing, I can't...

**L**oser attitude: I guess I'm nothing but a loser; I'll never amount to anything.

**D**oubting attitude: the number-one killer for success.

38

See how easily you can be drawn mentally into a negative belief system? That's why you must protect your backpack from negative intrusion.

Here's a quick test to see how you feel about yourself. Answer the following question: Do you like yourself? Yes or No?

Was your answer an immediate yes, or did you have to stop and think about it? Remember, if you don't like yourself then how can you expect others to like you? How do you see yourself every morning when you look in the mirror, providing you can look at yourself in the morning? Is your day just "another day, another dollar day" or is your day a special day to serve as an opportunity to better yourself? When you see yourself in the mirror, do you say to yourself: "God, what a great day I have ahead of me" or "Oh, my God, that's another day behind me"? Getting rid of negatives is very critical to your success.

After the Columbine shootings in Littleton, Colorado in April of 1999, I felt a tremendous responsibility to understand why school children want to shoot their classmates. As a motivational speaker to school children, I knew I would be asked about the shootings (and those which followed) by children who were concerned and fearful.

I am a parent myself, so I wanted to be prepared, to have answers, to reassure high schoolers, and my own children, that everything would be all right. I knew enough about human nature to know that human beings don't shoot each other in cold blood unless they are somehow dissociated (emotionally disconnected) from themselves and others. In each of the school shootings, the rage that the shootists felt would have to be *el grande* (huge, enormous) to plan and then carry out the mass executions of their schoolmates.

Then, almost a year later, in March of 2000, I read articles in *USA Today, Newsweek* and *Time* magazines summarizing a *CBS 60 Minutes II* segment on what the U.S. Secret Service found regarding the teenaged shooters. One report by CBS correspondent, Scott Pelley, said that "Many of (these teens) had considered suicide seriously, and many (said) that what brought them to that point was the malicious teasing in their school, which had gone on long enough."

We now know that some of the shooters shared their plans with classmates to justify their rage, and blamed their parents and teachers for not understanding their despondency, humiliation and anger. That kind of attitude is an extreme example of PLOM disease gone out of control. The young people who "pulled the trigger" saw themselves as victims. They defined their lives around their wounds and a sense of helplessness instead of seeking healing and positive outcomes. Their attitudinal lenses were colored with revenge and hate. They believed their victim status gave them a right to be manipulative, bitter and angry.

There are those who believe people are born with either good attitudes or bad attitudes. It would be nice if it were that simple. That's like saying some people are born to be stars, top athletes, leaders, top salespeople, top students, and so on. I would beg the difference with these folks. People who reach high levels of success in their chosen fields succeed because they pay their dues. They make conscious decisions to improve their natural talent. They develop positive attitudes and a strong sense of discipline to achieve their goals.

When things don't go the way we plan and we don't succeed at something, it is so easy to find fault in the system or blame others. We come up with reasons why we didn't achieve our goals. These reasons have a name. They're all called *excuses* and an excuse is the line of least *persistence*.

I have developed a visual aid for people who suffer from *excusitis*. Take a moment from your reading to make a small sign and place it in an open area of your home, class-room or work area. The small sign will read:

The journey from no excuses to results, from *victim* to *victor,* is a question of attitude – and attitudes are choices. It is true that attitudes are created by beliefs and beliefs, for the most part, are the result of socialization. But that doesn't alter the fact that you can over-ride that programming by exercising your power of choice. Your feelings, at any given moment and under any particular circumstance, are *always* determined by how you *choose* to feel. If you're into *woundology* or *victimology* and enjoy your PLOM disease status, you will choose to see everything from a victim standpoint.

There's a better way, of course. It happens to be a much brighter perspective. It's called positive thinking. It's trusting in your ability to turn trials into triumphs and vicious cycles into victories. Once you accept the fact that attitudes are choices and that you choose the way you think, act and feel, you will begin to achieve a level of success you previously thought was impossible.

People react to the list of situations below either positively or negatively. Decide how you feel about each of these examples as if you were experiencing them:

- Standing in line at the Post Office.
- Eating at an expensive restaurant.
- Catching a cold or the flu.
- Watching the evening news.
- Hearing a racist remark.
- Getting a haircut or manicure.
- Going to work.
- Listening to a chronic complainer.
- Drinking a cup of tea or coffee.
- Answering your e-mail.
- Making a mistake.
- Hearing someone talk about the corporate collapses.
- Having someone yell or scream at you.
- Playing with your favorite pet.
- Driving in inclement weather.
- Visiting the hospital.
- Shopping on the Internet.
- Wearing hand-me-down clothing.
- Being on the embarrassing end of a crude joke.
- Visiting family during your vacation.
- Hearing children at play.

Each of these 21 situations elicits feelings which can be either positive or negative. Would you feel victimized by any of these "events" if they happened to you or would you choose to feel triumphant? The choice is yours, of course. This was a simple "book" exercise; however, you have probably experienced each of these situations in "real" life. How will you react in the future? Will you see yourself as victim or victor?

# Be Sure to Unpack

There are some attitudes you can't afford to keep. They are toxic to your spirit and rob you of an immense amount of your energy – and health. Holding on to too many negative attitudes can be expensive – emotionally, mentally, physically and financially.

In the movie, *The Jerk*, Steve Martin plays an idiot who, through pure dumb luck, strikes it rich by inventing a unique handle for eyeglasses. He becomes a multimillionaire and indulges himself with every conceivable product on the market. He buys a huge mansion and fills it with his never-ending stream of purchases. As you've no doubt guessed, his life goes down the tube; his relationships fall apart, his luck takes a dive, his investments go south along with what is left of his self-esteem.

In a vintage Steve Martin comedic scene, he staggers through his mansion, intending to leave for good and boasting that he doesn't need anybody or anything. On the way out, however, he picks up a chair, a lamp, an article of clothing, a golf club and a vacuum cleaner.

"I don't need anything!" he bellows, "except this…and this…and this." By the time he trudges out the front door, he's burdened with a towering mountain of merchandise. All you can see of Steve are his legs, draped with his trousers which have fallen around his ankles. It is classic Steve Martin humor used to illustrate an important point about attitudes: carrying around too many useless attitudes can trip you up.

Attitudes like envy, resentment, selfishness, boredom, prejudice, contempt, guilt, doubt and distrust can lead to emotions such as fear, anger and rage. So often we weigh ourselves down with negative emotions and attitudes which trip us up, making our lives more complicated than they have to be. Duane Elgin reminds us in his insightful book *Voluntary Simplicity*, that:

> *We all know where our lives are unnecessarily complicated. We are all painfully aware of the distractions, clutter and pretense that weigh upon our lives and make our passage through the world more cumbersome and awkward. We must unburden our lives – to live more (purposefully) and unpretentiously.*

I'd like to use Steve Martin's movie to make one more point. Adopting negative attitudes, carrying them into your day and piling them into every situation and circumstance you encounter is the attitudinal equivalent of the Peter Principle. The Peter Principle says that people usually rise to their level of incompetence by being promoted to position after position until they end up with job responsibilities they cannot handle effectively. Sound familiar? You may know some people like that. You may even have found yourself in a position or two that tested your capabilities.

I believe people rise to their level of incompetence because they carry too many negative attitudes around with them. I may have stretched the analogy too far, but I don't think so. The toxicity of negative attitudes has been and continues to be one of the most researched areas in the success literature. When it is all said and done, successful people know that you can't manage your choices unless you manage your attitudes – and you can't manage your attitudes if you can't manage yourself. And you can't manage yourself until you unpack attitudes that don't work and repack your backpack with those that do.

As Zig Ziglar once put it, "Some folks just need a check-up from the neck-up." On the next page, I included a list which is your "check-up from the neck up." As quickly as you can, rate your attitude. The rating system is 1 to 5:

1. Poor

2. Needs Complete Overhaul

3. Needs Improvement

4. Good

5. Excellent

## Step Up and Measure Your Attitude

| | | | | | |
|---|---|---|---|---|---|
| 1. Your Self-Esteem | 1 | 2 | 3 | 4 | 5 |
| 2. Helping Others | 1 | 2 | 3 | 4 | 5 |
| 3. School | 1 | 2 | 3 | 4 | 5 |
| 4. Respecting Others | 1 | 2 | 3 | 4 | 5 |
| 5. Getting Help | 1 | 2 | 3 | 4 | 5 |
| 6. Responsibility | 1 | 2 | 3 | 4 | 5 |
| 7. Change | 1 | 2 | 3 | 4 | 5 |
| 8. Diversity | 1 | 2 | 3 | 4 | 5 |
| 9. Forgiveness | 1 | 2 | 3 | 4 | 5 |
| 10. Failure | 1 | 2 | 3 | 4 | 5 |
| 11. Family | 1 | 2 | 3 | 4 | 5 |
| 12. Your Job | 1 | 2 | 3 | 4 | 5 |
| 13. Studying | 1 | 2 | 3 | 4 | 5 |

I'm sure we can add more areas to this list, but this is a start, don't you agree? How did you do? Please relax. I've never met a "Perfect 5." Most people fall short in all of these areas. All of us need to improve our attitudes. How do we improve an attitude? Well, first we must get rid of the *bugs* in our lives. I believe *bugs* can destroy relationships, attitudes, classrooms, workplaces, teams and families. How much time does it take for this destruction? About ten seconds! When I use the word *bugs*, I'm not talking about cockroaches or some other type of insect that may give you the creeps. The *bugs* I'm referring to are four distinctive types of "attitudinal bugs."

> # B.U.G.S
>
> **Bitterness**
> **Unforgiveness**
> **Grudges**
> **Self-Righteousness**

I assure you that every one of us can relate to these *bugs*. Sad, but true. There are individuals that have been bitter for years, unwilling to forgive others and themselves. They hold grudges and hope someday they'll get even. Self-righteousness sets in where pride is not willing to give in.

Let me give you some exciting news. Your parents, siblings, relatives, teachers and employers aren't perfect! I hope you are smiling. I have better news for them. You are not perfect either. We all make mistakes. I like to use the phrase: all of us in one way or another have put our foot in our *la boca* (mouth) at one time or another. It's called foot-in-mouth disease. Since none of us is perfect and we all make mistakes, let's develop the right attitude and start getting rid of the *bugs* in our lives.

People who are bitter, unforgiving and waiting to get even are the most miserable, lonely and depressed folks I have ever met. There is a guarantee, my friend, you will be dead hundreds of years more than the few years you will be alive. So live your life pest-free. Turn what *bugs* you have into something that loves you.

After one of my presentations at a university where I spoke to 500 seniors, four young women came up to me. One of the ladies was crying, so I listened to her story.

She said, "You know, Mr. Jimmy, I am only 21 years old and the *bugs* have destroyed my family. I have not had any communication with my parents and I have been bitter against them for over five years. We had a major fight and they just #$%@^ me off."

Wow, at the age of 21, that five years represents a quarter of her life that she had not communicated with her parents. Isn't it sad that people put themselves through this kind of unnecessary stress and pain?

> *Thinking you can or thinking you can't takes up the same amount of energy.*

I challenged her to reconcile her differences by calling her parents immediately – collect of course. Thirty days later I received an email from her. She had made the call and resolved their differences. Everyone had forgiven each other. They had lifted tons of anger, pain, rejection and regrets from their backpacks. Who needs that kind of weight in their backpack? No one, wouldn't you agree?

I'm not perfect either. I've certainly made my share of mistakes – tons of them. I'm thankful my wife, children, friends and clients have forgiven me. At some of my presentations I challenge my audiences to go back to the office or classroom and wipe the slate clean. I believe it's never too late to forgive and bury grudges. Life is too short to live with such pain. We are here today and gone tomorrow, so it's time to get the *bugs* out.

> **A Backpack Keeper:** Forgiveness is faith in a hurry.

# Hola 100

Although the following statement has been around a long time, it is timeless and has much to say about the nature of success: Attitude is everything. *Everything* means 100% of something. Right! Using the 26 letter English alphabet to help make my point, I'm going to compare the impact of three powerful concepts: *hard work, knowledge* and *attitude.* Each letter of the alphabet has a corresponding number. "A" is the first letter so it gets a "1", "Z" is the 26th letter, so it equals the number 26. Let's complete the equation for all three concepts:

## Hard work :

H(8)+A(1)+R(18)+D(4)+W(23)+O(15)+R(18)+K(11)=98%

## Knowledge:

K(11)+N(14)+O(15)+W(23)+L(12)+E(5)+D(4)+G(7)+E(5)=96%

## Attitude:

A(1)+T(20)+T(20)+I(9)+T(20)+U(21)+D(4)+E(5)=100%

> **A Backpack Keeper:** A pinch of "possible" is worth more than a ton of logic.

# Backpack Wisdom

1. Attitude really is everything.

2. It's the choices we make and the attitudes that spawn them, not the circumstances we face, that determine our success or failure in life.

3. The journey from victim to victor is a question of attitude – and attitudes are choices.

4. You can't manage your choices until you manage your attitudes – and you can't manage your attitudes until you manage yourself.

5. Get the *bugs* out of your life. The pests I'm talking about are: **B**itterness, **U**nforgiveness, **G**rudges and **S**elf-Righteousness.

B

A

**C**ourage to Stretch Your Limits

K

P

A

C

K

# Chapter 3

# The Courage to Stretch Your Limits

*God, grant me the serenity to accept the things I cannot change, the courage to change the things I can, and the wisdom to know the difference.* (Serenity Prayer)

I can't think of a better way to open a chapter on courage than to honor the courageous acts of those brave Americans who gave their lives and risked their lives on September 11, 2001. In the space of one of those infamous "New York minutes," the lives of all Americans were changed forever. I know I'll never be the same. The staggering loss of lives at the World Trade Center, the Pentagon and Somerset County, Pennsylvania will forever be etched in our collective memories.

That morning, our daughter-in-law, Natalie, arrived to drop Tristan, our grandson, off for the day. She rushed into the house and told us to turn on the TV. That's how we found out about the attacks.

We saw planes slam into towering buildings and those same towering buildings collapse before our eyes; we saw the crash site of United Airlines Flight 93, a Boeing 757, near Pittsburgh; and we saw the incredible destruction of one whole wing of the Pentagon. For days, and even weeks, we were riveted to our TV sets as we followed the tragedy. We were inundated with the horrific images of death and destruction.

But, beyond the mass destruction, human suffering and death, those unspeakable acts carried with them something else – something that defines the extraordinary nature of the American spirit, something which separates us from those who hate freedom, something that reaches deep within every one of us who refuses to allow any act of terror to trump freedom and decency. That *something* is the extraordinary heroism of the firefighters, police officers, emergency service personnel, passengers on Flights 11, 77, 93 and 175, medical personnel, parks officers and victims at the disaster scenes. We've seen it before in our history – many times. I believe it's part of the helping nature of the human spirit. In the words of President George W. Bush, "In our grief and anger we have found our mission and our moment."

In a very real sense that's what this book is about - finding *your* mission and *your* moment. Courage comes in many forms. For a New York firefighter, it means rushing into a collapsing building. For cancer survivor Lance Armstrong, it means winning his fourth straight Tour de France. For Lisa Beamer, whose husband, Todd, helped rush the terrorists in the cockpit on United Flight 93, it means facing life and raising her children without her heroic husband. For someone else, it means saying "no" to drugs, alcohol, an abusive relationship, shyness, overeating, frivolous spending and a host of other habits or situations that attack our self-worth, health and happiness.

If you're like most of us, there have been times in your past – and maybe even now – that you've had to muster enough courage to step out of your comfort zone or face a life-defining challenge. All I know is that courage is a good thing to have in your backpack when you need it. It's that special *something* that resides deep within each of us that leaps out of us when the going gets tough. It's the part of us that refuses to bow to fear, force or foe. It's the part of us that, like Todd Beamer, says, "Are you ready guys? Let's roll."

Stepping out of our comfort zones can be risky business. I hope neither I nor you will ever have to rush terrorists in the cockpit of a 757 jet liner. Thankfully, most of our risks will not be life threatening in nature. Chances are, however, there will be times when we are pushed well outside of our comfort zones. When that happens, we will succeed or fail, depending on the choices we make.

> **A Backpack Keeper:** Courage is that special quality within us that refuses to bow to fear, force or foe.

# People Who Refused to Quit

I want to share a few stories of individuals who stepped out of their comfort zones and decided to take a certain amount of risk. The facts are true, only the identities of the people have been omitted. I am sure there are hundreds of stories like the ones I am sharing with you. These just happen to be some of my favorites. They have encouraged me to continue packing for success. I will reveal the people's names on page 58. Please don't read ahead until you finish all twelve snapshots. After reading each snapshot, decide if the individual in the example was a failure or success. Circle your response. Are you ready? Let's roll.

1. At Fort Necessity during the French and Indian War, this young American officer was soundly defeated and surrendered to the enemy. In fact, he lost more battles than he won during his military career. (Failure or Success?)

2. He had difficulty speaking. Even when he was asked the simplest question, his response was agonizingly slow. He just could not express himself. His parents had given up hope that he would ever reach the level of normal intelligence. They were told he would never amount to anything. (Failure or Success?)

3. He worked as a war correspondent and became a prisoner of war. He escaped, and after the war ended he decided he wanted to be a statesman and a military man. However, he lisped so badly that he was laughed off the platform when he made his first speech to the legislature. He failed three times to pass the entrance examination for the military academy. (Failure or Success?)

4. She wanted to be a performer and went to drama school in New York. After a few months, the school sent her home with a letter to her parents stating that they wasted their money because she had no talent or acting ability. Later she went back to New York and worked as a waitress to pay her own way through another drama school. She auditioned for numerous parts in small shows, but was always turned down. Meanwhile, she worked in a depart-

54

ment store as a clerk and in desperation accepted bit parts without pay just for the opportunity to be on stage. (Failure or Success?)

5. At age 14 he dropped out of school and hit the road. He tried jobs as a farmhand, streetcar conductor, blacksmith – and even studied law for a time, but failed in everything he attempted. He tried running a ferry boat, but was fired. He tried selling insurance. He sold tires. He was a fireman on a railroad loco-motive. Later he leased a small convenience store (in his day they were called filling stations) and added a small lunch counter to serve food to tourists. When a new highway was built around the small town, his convenience store was by-passed and he went broke. At age 65, all he had was his first month's Social Security check, no business, no job, no money and no property. (Failure or Success?)

6. He wanted to be an artist and went to Kansas City to apply for a job with one of the local newspapers. He was turned down by every newspaper and told that he didn't have any artistic talent. Everyone advised him to try something else. He lived in a dilapidated garage apartment that was infested with mice. Dur-ing his lifetime he went bankrupt seven times. (Failure or Success?)

7. He wanted to be in business for himself and served several years as an apprentice in a candy store. His family loaned him money to start a candy business in Philadelphia. After six years, he sold out and lost 96¢ on every dollar he had invested. The family agreed to help him start again and financed a Denver enterprise, but he ended up selling that business at a loss, too. The same thing happened in Chicago! His family disowned him and said he would never suc-

ceed. They refused to loan him any more money. He tried on his own in New Orleans and again in New York. It seemed as if he had the "minus" touch instead of a Midas touch. (Failure or Success?)

8. When he was six years old, he came home with a note from his teacher advising his parents that it was useless to keep him in the public school. He was diagnosed as too mentally retarded to learn. The parents were encouraged to commit him to a mental institution. (Failure or Success?)

9. Leslie went to school in Cleveland, Ohio. He wanted to be an entertainer, but had little experience and almost no training. He went to New York and the first time he walked out on stage, he was petrified! All of his reviews were poor. One reviewer wrote "If he is such a sensation in the Midwest, why doesn't he go back there? He has no talent and we don't want him here." (Failure or Success?)

10. This young man had a sparse work resumé and little more than a self-administered education. He tried to open a store, but went broke in just a few months. A year later he ran for the legislature, but was defeated. He tried to start another business, but went bankrupt. It took him 17 years to pay off his debts. He ran for public office and was defeated by a wide margin. He was defeated again six years later, but four years after that, he managed to get elected to Congress by a very close vote. He wanted to run for a second term, but his own party would not re-nominate him. He ran for the Senate twice, but was defeated both times. Altogether, he was defeated eight times in his attempts to be elected to public office. (Failure of Success?)

11. When he fell and scraped his knee in the stable yard one day, he was concerned that he had torn his only pair of trousers. His mother mended the trousers as well as she could and the 14-year-old forgot about his mishap. But the next day, he felt faint and feverish. He collapsed on the couch and drifted into delirium. Fearing for her son's life, his mother called the family doctor. After a brief examination, Dr. Conklin said her son had blood poisoning.

    During the following week, the doctor stopped by two to three times a day. He knew they were running out of options and that the boy was running out of time. Finally the doctor told his parents that his leg would have to be amputated. Half conscious, the boy overheard the doctor's prognosis. While his parents were in the next room discussing their options with the doctor, he asked his brother to promise him that he would never let them cut off his leg. Even when a consulting physician agreed that the boy's death was inevitable unless the leg came off, his brother stuck with his promise, and refused to allow them to do the amputation. (Failure or Success?)

12. This young man was born in a low socio-economic family in a time and area of Texas where the majority of people expressed their dislike for people of Mexican descent. At the age of 9, he thought about suicide. As a young man, he felt that the only way he would ever succeed in America was to be born white. In grade school he was rejected by his classmates and teachers. Throughout his public school experience, he felt he had only one friend. He wanted to try out for the drama team and join the choir, but he was not allowed to because of the color of his skin.

With no goals or dreams to speak of, he lived from day to day. To appease his parents he went to college, but two years later he was suspended because of his low grade point average. To avoid the draft, he joined the U.S. Navy. After his military duty, he tried unsuccessfully to find a civil service job. He found a job as a bartender on skid-row. When he realized that alcohol was taking control of his life, he sought another type of employment.

He tried a career in sales and in his first six months made a total income of $650. His manager and friends told him that he would never make it in sales and suggested he return to bartending. However, he persevered and after seven years in sales he announced he was going to become a professional speaker. His manager laughed at him. Four years later, he had delivered several hundred speeches before he was paid for the first one. (Failure or Success?)

How did you do on these snapshots? Count the number of failures and successes you circled.

Here's what is amazing: All of the individuals in these 12 snapshots became successful in their own right. They had the courage to step out of their comfort zones and take the kinds of risks that lead to positive outcomes. They were *backpack* people. Do you know who any of these people are?

### Answers to Success or Failure Exercise:

1. George Washington (First President); 2. Albert Einstein (Scientist); 3. Winston Churchill (Prime Minister of England); 4. Lucille Ball (*The I Love Lucy Show*); 5. Colonel Sanders (Kentucky Fried Chicken Founder); 6. Walt Disney (Disney World Founder); 7. Milton Hershey (Hershey Chocolate CEO); 8. Thomas Edison (Inventor); 9. Bob Hope (Actor/Comedian); 10. Abraham Lincoln (U. S. President); 11. Dwight Eisenhower (General and U. S. President); 12. Jimmy Cabrera, CSP (Professional Speaker and Consultant)

> **A Backpack Keeper:** Do not be fooled by the "scarecrow power" of uncertainty.

# Exaggerate the Positive

The willingness to confront fear is called courage. Cora Harris, a superb author, puts it this way. "The bravest thing you can do when you are not brave is to profess courage and act accordingly." I like the idea of professing courage, because the very act of doing something to combat your fears helps you to move beyond the paralysis that would otherwise immobilize you. It is this immobilization that makes fear so debilitating.

I'm going to toss a concept at you. You may have heard of it; however, if you haven't, it'll help you understand the extraordinary power you can have over anything that frightens you. It's a concept called "learned helplessness."It involves the immobilizing effects that panic has on our brain chemistry. It seems that the mere perception of an event as being beyond our control predisposes us to give up emotionally so that we literally choose helplessness over action. It is not the exposure to a stressful experience itself that causes us to shut down, but the perception of our total lack of control over real or imagined dangers.

So many of our fears are unfounded. They are emotional phantoms which rarely exist in reality. Some people invent fearful situations and succumb to fearful attitudes to avoid taking responsibility for their thoughts and actions. They usually repeat statements like: "I'll never get out of this mess," or "I can't stand all of this stress. I'm feeling so overwhelmed," or "This is impossible. There's no way out of this."

People who disempower themselves using excuses like these are "exaggeration experts" – but they exaggerate the wrong thing! They over-dramatize the negative aspects of the simplest challenges in life. Anything out of the ordinary is upsetting to them. They intentionally over-burden themselves with a backpack full of negatives and are usually very good at creating situations that prove they are being victimized by life in general.

> *It is easy for others to tell you what to do because they don't have to worry about the consequences you have to face when you make that decision.*

As you have noticed, I have included personal stories about myself and my family in this book. I have chosen to share them because my life is an open book. I won't withhold anything I believe will help you become a *backpack* person. Our family's experiences mirror many families' experiences. The important thing is that we have the courage to share our family narratives so someone else can be helped – and encouraged.

The following story is about my daughter, Alétta. When Alétta was seventeen, her mother, Laural, and I discovered she was experimenting with drugs. I have Alétta's permission to share her story just as I have her sister, Chambray's, permission to share one about her later. Alétta had experimented with marijuana before she "graduated" to the hard stuff.

We almost lost her one night when she took not one, but two taps of Acid. Her hallucinations were horrific. Her despair, pain and dishevelment frightened us, but we were just as concerned about her emotional and spiritual ailments. We also felt guilty and embarrassed – and angry –

that our lovely seventeen-year old daughter had made such a disastrous, life-threatening choice.

She told us she would never experiment with drugs again, and she has kept her word. She has been drug-free for over eight years. We are so proud of her. She told us that there were three major reasons why she quit using drugs: She did it for herself and her own health and well-being; she knew her mother and I would never compromise our values at home and allow her to stay under the same roof if she continued to experiment with drugs; and she got very frightened of the tremendous power of the drugs which had taken such total control of her life. She vowed that she would never again put herself in a position in which she was not in total control of her faculties.

Laural and I have thanked Alétta many times over these past eight years for having the courage to accept the consequences of her actions, learning from her mistakes and making the kind of positive life-affirming decisions that make her an extraordinary *backpack* person. (Alétta, your mother and I thank you again for allowing me to include your story so that others will be encouraged to follow your example by staying drug-free.)

The word "drugs" tells quite a sad story:

**D**oubting reality

**R**egretting the consequences

**U**ncertain about the future

**G**utter is where you will end up

**S**elf-pity is the #1 reason for taking drugs

The reality is drugs will thrill you
until they kill you.

Fortunately, human beings have the incredible power to take any experience and learn from it or allow it to limit their ability to go on. *Backpack* people have faith that there is a reason for the unexplainable and the unknowable, the tragic and the challenging. The need to believe in positive outcomes and lasting recovery is essential to our health and well-being. The distinguished Norman Cousins used a medical metaphor: "Drugs are not always necessary, (but) belief in recovery always is." Norman Cousins was a *backpack* person. He realized that we must have the courage to believe because our beliefs have as much to do with our cures as medicine. In a very real sense, positive, life affirming beliefs are our medicine.

My daughter, Chambray's story is similar to her sister's in one respect and quite different in another. Like her sister, she summoned the courage to admit her mistake, suffered the consequences without complaint, and took full responsibility for her actions. Her life lesson was different in the respect that it involved shoplifting, not drugs. She was caught trying to steal a $20 blouse.

Although it was her first – and subsequently only – offense, Chambray could have spent six months in jail. Fortunately, her penalty was reduced to one year's probation, 50 hours of community service and a 10 p.m. curfew for one year (her senior year in high school). Because of the restrictions, Chambray missed many of her senior class activities, but she honored the court order and learned important lessons from her shoplifting experience. She told us, "Dad, Mom, some of my classmates think like I did, that they won't get caught. Remind them in your book and in your speeches that they will get caught and that it's not worth it."

Her mother and I thank our Lord for allowing Chambray to get caught the first time she broke the law. We also thank Him for His mercy and allowing her to learn a very important lesson without having to pay too high a price.

Chambray has added the courage of her convictions to her backpack of life. Alétta has added it to her backpack, too.

Neither of our daughters disempowered themselves by manufacturing excuses to justify their actions. Neither exaggerated her dilemma by over-dramatizing the negative aspects of her predicament or over-reacting to the consequences. Instead, both of our daughters displayed an amazing amount of courage and common sense, and exaggerated the positive. They are better people because of the experience and we are a better family for having gone through it together.

> **A Backpack Keeper:** There are two lasting gifts we can give our children.
> One is a solid foundation.
> The other is wings.

## ʟighten Your ʟoad

In *The White Hole in Time*, Peter Russell explains:

*The heaviest burdens in this life are not our physical burdens, but our emotional ones. We weigh ourselves down with our concerns for the past and our worries about the future. This is the load we bear, the weariness that comes from our timefulness…We must relieve ourselves of this load.*

I promised Laural I'd tell this story on myself because it shows that it's never too late to be courageous enough to ask for forgiveness. It also demonstrates the power of an individual's influence on others. As a Freshman in high school, I was good in track and field events. I was a fairly good track star. They called me Speedy Gonzales, but I didn't mind – because I was very fast and I was very Mexican. One day our coach conducted try-outs for a four-member relay team. I was fortunate enough to make the relay team, but unfortunate enough to have made an enemy. One of the students I had taken a relay spot from was a Junior who had previously been a member of the relay team. He was extremely unhappy about losing his spot – especially to a Mexican. He made his sentiments known to everyone and proceeded to make my life as miserable as he could.

Although I fielded his displeasure with as much tact and diplomacy as I could, I refused to give up my spot on the relay team – to him or anyone else. If they wanted my spot, they would have to better my time. My parents told me, "Son, in life you will have to learn to make the dust or you will eat the dust." So, for the next two years, that negative person ate my dust.

Years later I attended my 20th class reunion. Classes of '61 through '66 held their class reunion as a team reunion. Of all the people at the reunion, guess who I ran into? You guessed it. The Junior who had made my life so miserable in high school. He asked me if we could talk privately. I agreed, and he proceeded to tell me how much he admired me.

"You know, Jimmy," he said, "back in high school you and your family weathered a lot of prejudice, and I must admit, I was one of the worst offenders. I'm a principal now at a small middle school near Dallas. I remember your strong character and how you never wavered from your principles.

"So now, at the beginning of each school year, I gather all the students in the auditorium for an assembly on the Pillars of Character and Success. I tell a story about a young student who happened to be of Mexican descent. I explain how his strength of character and the character of his family influenced me to change the way I felt about other cultures. I encourage them to treat others with dignity and respect. I assure each of them that they can learn a lot from other people and especially other cultures. I tell them how much I learned from that young track star and how I admired his courage. Jimmy, that young track star was you. Can you find it within your heart to forgive me?"

I must admit, I was speechless. I thought no one ever noticed or paid attention to me. What a great confirmation to realize that each and every one of us can be a role model to someone if we have the courage to stand for our convictions. As a direct result of that conversation, I brainstormed a list of courageous acts that I could share with my audiences. I have added a few courageous acts to that list over the years. What follows is the culmination of my efforts to generate a meaningful list of random acts of courage.

### It takes courage to:

| | |
|---|---|
| Stay in school | Continue your education |
| Have integrity | Seek counsel |
| Ask for help | Voice your opinion |
| Stand for what you believe in | Take responsibility |
| Be intellectually curious | Mature responsibly |
| Test assumptions | Remain teachable |
| Be a team player | Receive criticism |
| Admit your mistakes | Make decisions |
| Forgive yourself and others | Have a positive attitude |
| Set goals | Believe in yourself |
| Have strong moral values | Succeed without complaining |
| Volunteer in your community | Seek spiritual direction |
| Take advice willingly | Dream big |
| Hold your head high | Get out of your comfort zone |

Think things through before you decide

I want to add one more to the list and I believe it will strengthen and support them all. That is having the courage to **never lose hope!**

Unpacking emotional fears and doubts has a physiological counterpart. Physiologists and immunologists have known this for years. Every cell in our bodies, from our facial muscles to the interior lining of our hearts, stomachs and lungs, contains receptor sites for the chemicals involved in our emotions. I mention this because there has been some astounding medical research over the last couple of years confirming that our emotions affect us biochemically, touching every cell and molecule in our makeup.

Within the brain, the chemicals that affect our moods, thoughts and attitudes are called *neuropeptides*. In the rest of the body they are called *peptides*. Even the *lymphocytes*, the cells of the immune system, contain receptor sites for fielding our emotions. Every emotion has its own chemical signature. By an act of choice we can create angelic reactions at a cellular level or produce monstrous reactions which deplete our vitality and sew cords of distress and disease.

> **A Backpack Keeper:** When you are faced with a parade of problems, it's better to fall flat on your face than bow to expediency.

## Never Lose Hope

Occasionally I run into a few seniors in high schools who ask me, "Why go to college? There's no future for our generation?"

My response is very simple, "What are you talking about? You are the future."

Unfortunately, there are many individuals of all ages that have lost hope. A friend of mine, Barry, got my attention when he said, "With the loss of hope, comes the hope of death." It's a heavy statement, but it has to be made to encourage every human being to never lose hope. In my backpack of life, I make sure I pack so much hope that it overflows. Let me explain what I mean.

As I described earlier in this book, I grew up in a time when racial prejudice defined our society. I felt like an outcast – unwanted, unappreciated and unloved – except by my family. During one of my soul-searching moments, I was so despondent and depressed that I thought about suicide. I was only nine at the time, but self-annihilation seemed like the perfect solution. I decided to try one more thing which I felt would help me "fit in" at school before I attempted the unspeakable. I had entertained thoughts of "checking out"…thoughts of suicide. My brothers were at school, dad was at work and I thought my mom was visiting a friend across the street. In reality she was in the next room.

Although I didn't quite know how I was going to dispose of myself, I knew I had to do something drastic to change my identity so the other kids would accept me. So I went into the kitchen and heated a small pot of water. Then I retrieved a bar of soap and scrub brush and started scrubbing my face, arms and hands. In my 9-year old mind, I figured I could scrub my brown Mexican skin off so I would be white. If I were white-skinned, I reasoned, I'd be accepted by my classmates.

The scrubbing, of course, turned my skin red and raw instead of white. So, I decided to stick to my original plan and dispose of myself.

"I'm not worth anything to anybody," I said out loud. "Why should I go on living? Maybe I should hang myself. No, that would hurt. Maybe I should cut my wrists…no, my mom would probably make me clean up the mess."

I was totally caught off guard when my mother said: "What did you say?"

I said, "Mom, I don't want to live."

She slapped me across my face and said, "I didn't hear you."

And again I said, "Mom, I don't want to live."

WHOP! The sound of her slapping me again! I hesitated before I spoke, then exclaimed, "Mom, I think I want to live!" That's when she grabbed me and kissed me.

Then she shook me. "Don't you ever say that again," she screamed. Then she lifted me onto the table and steeled her gaze on me. There was fire in her eyes. "Do you hear me? Don't you ever say that again."

She told me how special I was and how much she loved me. She reminded me how smart I was and how sensitive I was to other people's feelings.

Then she buried my head into her bosom and said, "*Dios no hace basura.*" (God doesn't make any junk.)

From that moment on, I have never thought of suicide again. I can vividly remember every word she said, the way the room looked and the smells that permeated the house. I also remember the fiery look in her eyes. It was a look which said: *How dare you think so little of yourself. You are priceless. You are unique. You are special. You will be successful one day if you give yourself a chance.*

I never questioned my value after that day, and I knew two very important things: Mom loved me and God doesn't make any junk. I remember looking at my hands and arms. *God made my skin brown*, I remember thinking, *so brown must be okay because God doesn't make mistakes. And I'm not a mistake either.*

> **God doesn't make any junk.**

People ask me why I share this story. I want everyone to know that they are special and that suicide is NEVER the answer. In the last ten years I have presented in over 700 schools. When I first spoke in schools, I asked the students a specific question after I had gotten permission from the school administration. I would ask how many students ever thought about suicide. Ten years ago no more than 1% of the audience would openly admit that they thought of suicide. Recently at a school assembly, I asked the same question and over 10% of the audience openly admitted such thoughts. As of this writing, one high school in America has witnessed four suicides in the last ten months.

I advise all of my student audiences that suicide is never the answer to their problems. The correct solution is seeking help from a school counselor, a friend, parent, pastor, priest, rabbi, or clinical psychologist. I encourage them to talk to someone about their feelings, and to explain what they may be going through. I tell them everyone has problems. Everyone gets knocked down or tripped up. I tell them sometimes it seems as if you can't depend on anyone – but God – and God doesn't make junk.

I have been fortunate to have received many letters from students who have thanked me for giving them hope and helping them believe that they aren't junk. (See Chapter Nine.) I tell them they have value and that everyone has a purpose.

Just this last year a teenager approached me after one of my presentations and said, "Mr. Jimmy, I want you to know that I planned to say good-bye to this world this week. And today after school I was ready to kill myself. I did not want to attend this assembly. But I am glad I did. After hearing your program, I don't want to take my life. I want to become a *backpack* person. Thank you for coming to our school. Thank you for saving my life."

Personal encounters like this help me to know that I'm in the right business. I feel so privileged to be able to help people become *backpack* people. Their stories have touched me deeply and their capacity to turn their lives around is nothing short of phenomenal.

> **Never deprive people of hope; it may be all they've got to hang onto.**

I'd like to tell you about one of the techniques I use to remind people of the importance of hope. On the back of one of your business cards, a wallet-sized photo, a post-it-note, or a 2x3 inch piece of paper, I want you to write the word **HOPE**. Then sign it and date it with today's date. Keep it in your wallet or purse along with your driver's license and credit cards.

Whenever you experience adversity or lose hope, I want you to pull out your "Hope Card" to remind yourself that no matter what you are going through, there's always hope. Shortly before this book was published, I met my friend, Joel, for lunch. Part of our discussion involved uplifting some of our mutual friends who were going through tough times in this post-9/11 economy. At one point, he reached into his wallet and pulled out his "Hope Card" and said, "Jimmy, eleven years ago I attended one of your presentations and you challenged our group to keep our "Hope Cards" in good standing. Well, here's my card and I can't tell you how many times I've pulled it out of my wallet. See, you can tell it's been used quite a lot."

A few years ago I received a letter from a student that truly encourages me to continue to make a difference in the lives of others. I know the letter by heart:

*Dear Mr. Cabrera,*

*My name is Gina and I am 12 years old and in the seventh grade. Thank you for coming to my school. I liked your presentation and learned a lot. I have an A.L.L. type cancer but I will never give up. I will remember the things you said and when I don't feel good before or after chemo, I will look at the piece of paper I wrote hope on and I promise that I will never give up. I hope you can come back to our school and give another speech.*

*Sincerely,*
*Gina*

Wow, that my friends, wouldn't you agree, is an awesome letter? Whenever I experience a bad day, all I have to do is read some of the letters I have received. The last chapter of this book is a compilation of some of the letters I have received through the years that encourage me and give me a *faith-lift* when I need it. I hope they will inspire you, too! Before I close out this section on hope, I want to tell you the rest of Gina's story.

Three years after I first met Gina, I was invited back to her school. She was sitting in the front row. I was told her cancer was in remission. I was so moved that I pulled the letter she had written to me three years earlier out of my suit coat pocket – and read it to the entire student body. It was one of the most heart-felt moments I have ever experienced on the platform. Fifteen hundred students gave Gina a standing ovation.

Three years after that second encounter, I experienced an even greater moment. The Senior Class at that same school invited me to deliver the keynote address at their graduation ceremony. I accepted and on graduation day, I prepared to address 3,000 people in a sports arena packed to capacity. The students surprised me by having Gina introduce me.

I make my living as a keynote speaker, but I can tell you I was so filled with emotion that I was speechless. After a couple of minutes, I regained my composure and delivered my speech. My opening remarks included a special thanks to Gina for exemplifying hope and courage and for affirming my belief in the human spirit. Then I reminded the seniors to fill their backpacks with the right stuff and prepare for the challenges of adult life.

> **A Backpack Keeper:** Hope has
> both push and pull.

## The Fear Factor

"It's alive!" That is what mad scientist, Victor Frankenstein exclaimed in James Whale's black-and-white 1931 version of the classic film *Frankenstein's Monster,* immortalized by Boris Karloff's stunning performance as the sewn-together, freakish "monster." Unfortunately, we create the same kind of molecular nightmare every time we allow fear to immobilize us. Our challenge is to see fear for what it is. "**F**alse **E**vidence **A**ppearing **R**eal. That acronym for "FEAR" has been around a long time, but its truth deserves to be repeated. Recognizing how the demoralizing effects of fear could ruin a nation, our thirty-second President, Franklin Delano Roosevelt told us over fifty years ago:*"The only thing we have to fear is fear itself – nameless, unreasoning, unjustified terror which paralyzes needed efforts to convert retreat into advance..."*

> **If we are consumed by fear, we can be bankrupt of courage.**

Fear has a purpose. It alerts us to danger and prepares our bodies for fight or flight. The fear response goes something like this. When you are frightened, you feel an immediate rush of adrenaline. Your brain alerts your body that it believes you are in imminent danger. It does this with a thought and then a signal through neurotransmitters. Immediately, the brain orders extra supplies of oxygen and adrenaline throughout your entire body by increasing your heart rate. This increased heart rate is called tachycardia and is perfectly normal when you are frightened.

Adrenaline rushes blood to your extremities (hands, arms, legs and feet) because the muscles in these areas need extra strength. This is an automatic response because our extremities are our physiological line of defense from attack. Adrenaline also inhibits pain. So in the "heat of battle" you may not feel the pain initially caused by a wound until the harmful episode – real or imagined – is over.

Your breathing also becomes faster and more shallow. Your shoulders become more tense and tight. The synapses in your brain are firing neuro-signals to every part of your body. Your emotional antennae are on full alert. Sometimes fear and worry use up this energy so fast that you feel drained or even exhausted. Some people feel a sense of hopelessness, doom or despair.

The reason the "fear factor" is so important to our discussion is that fear tends to immobilize us instead of acting to empower us over what we perceive to be a dangerous or threatening situation. It keeps us from taking risks and welcoming changes that can enhance the quality of our lives. If we are consumed by fear, we can be bankrupt of courage. Most fears are irrational. They are contrary to reason and common sense. They usually have no basis in reality. The chances of the fearful thing actually occurring, although within the realm of possibility, are highly improbable.

> **The chance of a fearful event actually occurring is highly unlikely.**

It takes courage to face your fears. I certainly don't want to suggest that fears, even irrational fears, should be taken lightly. But I can tell you this in all sincerity – *backpack* people have learned to supplant fear with courage. Whether it's fear of loss of control, abandonment, lengthy illness, death, suffering, financial ruin, criticism or speaking in public (which is the number one fear in America, believe it or not) – its effects are demoralizing and immobilizing.

There are some courageous steps you can take to move beyond your fears. I'd like to suggest a few:

1. Get clear in your own mind what you are really afraid of and determine as best you can whether that fear is rational or irrational.

2. Talk to other people who have similar fears to gain insights, advice and direction. Talk to trusted friends, people with whom you feel comfortable sharing such personal information.

3. Write or type a letter to your fears. I'm serious. Tell your fear how you feel about it. Explain why you are so afraid of it and how it immobilizes you. Ask it to help you become less afraid. Tell it you know it's

here to teach you a lesson, to help you understand yourself better. Forgive it for frightening you. Ask it to be your friend. Ask it for a solution to your fearfulness.

4. Work on overcoming a particular fear by gradually exposing yourself to it. Ask a trusted friend and/or a professional therapist to help you tame the fear. Take it a step at a time so you can build confidence as you go. Reward yourself, for each small successful step.

5. Ask yourself why this particular fear is an issue. Are you using it as an excuse not to move forward in an important area in your life? Are you avoiding growth or responsibility in a critical lifestyle area? What is it about this particular fear that makes you feel so powerless and helpless?

6. Visualize yourself overcoming this fear. See successful outcomes in your mind's eye. Repeat positive affirmations like: "If it is to be, it is up to me."

7. Send plenty of *knee-mail* to God. Knee-mail is prayer. Spending time on my knees is one of the best antidotes I know to solve any human dilemma. I have found regular and systematic prayer to be a wonderful *faith-lift*.

8. Realize that you have the capacity to overcome any fear and obstacle in life. No problem, no handicap, no disability, no fearful possibility can intimidate you without your consent. So don't give it! Use your God-given power of choice to turn your fears into friends.

Dr. Lila Swell describes it this way in her book, *Success: You Can Make It Happen.* "Once you know your needs, you also have to feel entitled to meet those needs, you will make self-fulfilling rather than self-defeating choices." Success, she believes, happens when the choices we make bring positive experiences that shape our lives. Success and happiness are not matters of chance, but choice.

Once you choose to move beyond your fears and move decisively toward your dream, you will meet with the level of success you are willing to settle for. One thing is for certain, and you can take this to the bank – if you really want to succeed, you can always find a capable, committed and helping hand at the end of your own sleeve! In my business, I often see people who do not succeed, but I rarely see anyone who cannot succeed.

> **A Backpack Keeper:** Face fear by flaunting your courage.

## The Amazing Z Effect

You've heard the expression, "Feel the fear and do it anyway." I'm a big believer in that philosophy. Fear is a natural – and controllable – emotion. Face your fears, using all the help and guidance you need. It is important for you to do what Eleanor Roosevelt advised us to do so many years ago: "You must do the thing you think you cannot do."

An analogy I've found especially helpful when it comes to conquering fear is the "suspended foot" metaphor. Each step we take involves a suspended foot as we step on one foot and lift the other to take the next step forward. If we identify all of our progress with the suspended foot – we may panic, believing we aren't on solid ground. But if we focus on the relationship between the two feet, we realize that we have one foot supporting us all the time.

A perfect illustration of "feel the fear and do it anyway" comes from the hilariously entertaining Steven Spielberg movie, *The Mask of Zorro*. Antonio Banderas stars as the masked hero and Catherine Zeta-Jones plays Elena, the film's beautiful female lead. In one flamboyant scene, Zorro outwits Elena in a lightly romantic interlude that shows how masterful the masked marvel can be in combat:

> *Zorro says to her: "Do you surrender?"*
> *"Never! But I may scream!" Elena answers.*
> *"I understand," quips Zorro, "I sometimes have that effect on people."*

Although she was frightened – "I may scream" – Elena was determined to hold her ground. She was a lovely example of courage under fire. She was prepared to "do the thing she thought she could not do." Of course, she was only playing a part in a movie, but she exemplifies what I call "The Z Effect" – the mark of Zorro. Just like Zorro, Elena left her mark on a frightening situation. A mark that says, "I'm frightened, but I'm going to do this anyway." A mark that leaves an indelible imprint of courage and character on a frightful situation.

With three lightning fast strokes of his saber tip – *swit, swit, swit* – the masked caballero leaves his Z slash as evidence of his presence. But it means more, much more than that. The mark of Zorro is the mark of courage, class and charm over any power, force or situation that seeks to minimize human worth and potential.

> **Feel the fear, but do it anyway.**

## Swit, Swit, Swit

There's no time like the present to leave your mark on a fearful or frightening personal limitation. Find a red-inked pen or colored marker and complete the following exercise:

Evaluate this list of fears common to most people. To the left of each fear is a box. For each fear you believe is not a fear for you or is one you have overcome, place a Z in the box next to it. Use a little flare as you slash the Z's across the boxes. You can begin to slash your fears below:

❑    Fear of speaking in public.

❑    Fear of loss of control.

❑    Fear of a long-term debilitating illness or accident.

❑    Fear of dying.

❑    Fear of criticism.

❑    Fear of public embarrassment.

❑    Fear of financial ruin.

❑    Fear of losing something or someone you love.

❑    Fear of the dark.

❑    Fear of small, tight, cramped spaces.

❑    Fear of drowning.

❑    Fear of snakes.

❑    Fear of flying.

❑    Fear of heights.

If you leave any unslashed boxes, I recommend your doing something about those fears. Review the steps you can take to move beyond your fears in the "Fear Factor" section on pages 74 and 75 in this chapter. That should give you a good start.

Remember no fear can intimidate you without your consent.

When Elena faced Zorro, she stood on her own two feet. She didn't identify herself with a suspended foot. Although she wasn't absolutely sure, she had faith that the masked man who stood confidently before her would not harm her. She might scream, but she would not surrender.

Faith involves letting go – that's the suspended foot. Fear holds on. It wants guarantees. Fear is unsure of life, but faith is full of life. The courage to step out on life, to suspend guarantees, and at the same time believe that all things work together for good is the *backpack* philosophy of life.

> **A Backpack Keeper:** Punch and kick your way out of any adversity – use your backpack black belt in courage.

# Backpack Wisdom

1. Courage is that special something that resides deep within each of us that refuses to bow to fear, force or foe.

2. Unpacking is as important as packing.

3. Some people disempower themselves by exaggerating the impact of everyday life experiences.

4. Our challenge is to see fear for what it is: **F**alse **E**vidence **A**ppearing **R**eal.

5. You have the capacity to overcome any fear and obstacle in your life.

6. When it comes to guaranteeing your success, you can always find a capable, committed and helping hand at the end of your own sleeve.

7. Fear is unsure of life, but courage is self-affirming and self-fortifying.

B

A

C

Knowledge Sought and Applied

P

A

C

K

# Chapter 4

# Knowledge Sought and Applied

*Apply yourself. Get all the knowledge you can, but then, do something about it. Don't just stand there, make it happen.* (Lee Iacocca)

I am a firm believer in the fact that our self-development limits are our ego's limits. When we move beyond rigid ego boundaries, we open ourselves up to unlimited possibilities in all areas of our lives. Permit me to share a well-known story that illustrates this point. It is the story of a learned university professor who was a respected school administrator, excelling in strategic planning.

*A young professor decided to visit a wise old retired administrator who had a similar specialty. The young professor was writing a book and wanted to ask the old mentor a few questions and discuss several curiosities.*

*The old man received the self-assured professor in his library, and an attendant served tea. As soon as the young professor seated himself, he began boasting about his academic success, his considerable administrative credentials and his expertise in their shared field. The old administrator said nothing as he poured tea into his boastful guest's cup. The young professor hardly noticed the old man's hospitality and kept talking about his own accomplishments.*

*Suddenly the young professor realized that his host was still pouring tea into an already overflowing cup. The hot tea was spilling over the table and onto the hardwood floor.*

*"Stop," cried the professor. "What are you doing? You're spilling all of the tea."*

*The old administrator looked at his puzzled colleague and smiled softly.*

*"Just as the cup cannot hold anymore tea once it's filled," he replied, "how can I give you the information you need when your ego is so full?"*

As the old administrator demonstrated so dramatically, we cannot listen to anyone else's advice or wise counsel if we are full of ourselves. The young professor in this story seemed to be "full of himself." He was egotistical and egocentric. More than likely, he never talked about anyone else because he always talked about himself. He certainly was not ecumenical in praising others or listening to their advice.

Someone once told me that *EGO* means "Edging God Out." I think that applies to people who can't keep their egos in check. All of us have egos and most people have healthy egos. A healthy ego contributes to a high level of self-esteem and confidence in oneself. Each of us has a distinct personality and our ego is the conscious connection between our self-concept and the other people around us. Our energies are usually directed toward realizing our own potentials and achieving our own goals. Like the misguided young professor, some people create and protect a false, idealized self which is based on pride and self-preservation. They seek the advice and counsel of knowledgeable people, but feel threatened at the same time. Like the professor, they use ego-centrism and pride as defense mechanisms to protect their fragile egos.

---

### *Negative EGO:*

**Edge God Out**
**Edge the Good Out**
**Everyone's Got One**

---

No matter how well educated you are and how much expertise you acquire in a certain area, there's always more to learn. People who remain teachable are the ones who maximize their success in life.

They are careful not to let pride get in their way. They are *backpack* people. They recognize that our egos influence our behavior more than any other single factor in our make-up. It is our chief perceptual filter. We perceive the world – its events, objects and people – through the ego's lens of the world. Great leaders like Bill Gates, Margaret Thatcher, Fred Smith, Colin Powell and President George W. Bush know how to keep their egos in check. They know they have more to learn and hire trusted advisors to keep them informed.

> **A Backpack Keeper:** Many people know
> what to do, but few people have
> the commitment and common
> sense to do what they know.

# Seek Profound Knowledge

For most of my life, I have sought what the internationally famous management consultant, D. W. Edwards Deming, calls "profound knowledge." To me, profound knowledge is applied expertise, strategy, techniques and experience that improve our present and future chances of success.

This book and my entire speaking career are public demonstrations of my commitment to give others the *right* knowledge to pack in their backpacks of life. It is my sincere desire that you apply the techniques you learn in this book. Learn as much as you can about things which will take you one step closer to your goal.

> *The more we learn, the more we realize how little we actually know.*

Be good at something that brings you joy and helps people. Competence breeds confidence and vice-versa. We are all good at something. Over the years of my speaking career, I have presented to doctors, lawyers, engineers, bankers, teachers, students, administrators, psychologists, college presidents, CEOs, housewives, sales people, healthcare professionals, church boards, and many other fine people in wonderful professions. No matter who it is or what my audiences do for a living, I find myself saying to myself, *These people know so much more than I do about what they do.* I hold my audiences in the highest regard for their expertise in their chosen fields.

Because I prepare for my presentations in advance by interviewing the meeting planner and key members of the company, school or association, I gain a snapshot appreciation for what my audiences do for a living and the challenges which face them. But they are the experts, not me. However, I am an expert at what I do for a living, and part of my responsibility as a speaker is to make my expertise relevant to the needs of my audiences.

> ## *No acquired knowledge is wasted unless it isn't applied.*

I must admit, when I was young I wasn't a very good reader, nor did I care to read books. I don't recall reading a single book in its entirety in school or out of school.

A very dear friend and mentor, George Roach, was influential in getting me to make a positive decision about reading. In the fall of 1974 I had just entered the sales industry as a salesperson. I'd stop by his place of business and he'd take a few minutes to talk with me about sales and marketing. On one such visit our conversation was about self-improvement books on leadership, sales and marketing. He asked me names of books I had read on any of these topics. When I told George about my anti-reading pilgrimage through life, he couldn't believe it.

He said, "You know, Jimmy, if you elect not to read, you are as bad off as the person who cannot read at all."

---

**If you read nothing, you are nothing.**

---

Hello, Earth to Jimmy. I must admit his advice got my attention. You may be familiar with the old adage, *When the student is ready, the teacher will arrive.* His wisdom awakened me and ever since that day, I have never been the same. When I left George's office, I stopped by the nearest book store and purchased my first book. At the ripe old age of 29, I read my first book, cover to cover, word for word. This experience changed my life. The book was by Maxwell Maltz, *Psycho Cybernetics.* In fact, it took me a long while to finish reading the book, with the assistance of Webster. I also attended various self-help and sales educational workshops, and took advantage of books and seminars by Dale Carnegie, J.D. Edwards, Zig Ziglar, Tom Hopkins, Napoleon Hill, Norman Vincent Peale, Earl Nightingale, Cavett Robert and many more.

One of the workshops was conducted by Charlie "Tremendous" Jones. At one point in his program he grabbed a box full of books and dumped its contents onto the stage. Books went everywhere. After the initial shock, the entire room became silent. You could hear a pin drop. Then he said, "You are and will become what you read." Hmmmmm, maybe it's time to check the things we read? May I add that if you read nothing, you are nothing. Ouch!

**A Backpack Keeper:** If you choose not to read, you are as bad off as the person who cannot read at all.

# Applied Knowledge is Power

Dr. Lassiter, president of a college where I was invited to present, gave me some unique words of wisdom that he learned from this father,· "If you want to get ahead, put something in your head." Dr. Lassiter understood the value of learning and the necessity of putting the right knowledge in your head.

> **If you want to get ahead,**
> **put something in your head.**

I realize you've probably heard this before, but I want to remind you one more time: Education is a major key to your success. With education comes knowledge. You can take "things" away from me, but there is one *thing* you can never take away – the knowledge I put into my head. You may be familiar with the phrase "knowledge is power," but my question to you is this: Do you believe that knowledge is power?

Well, I don't believe knowledge is power. The pursuit of knowledge just for the sake of knowledge is useless and will leave us empty. Allow me to explain. Success occurs when we add **ac** to the word **knowledge**. Success comes when we *acknowledge* that **applied knowledge is power.**

Note the difference in the two statements. You can know more about a subject, topic or procedure than any other person, but until you apply that knowledge, it will not help you move forward to ensure greater outcomes.

Education gives us a better understanding of how things work and get done. It provides access to more opportunities. We have entered the 21st Century. We can choose whether or not we want to be better educated.

At a school assembly during one of my presentations, I made the following bold statement: "How many of you would like to guarantee that if you follow four simples rules, you will pass every subject in school?"

You should have seen the response when 100% of the students raised their hands. The four rules are:

## 1. Never be ashamed to ask for help.

When do you think the average person stops asking for help? In my opinion we stop asking for help in the second or third grade. Why? That is usually when we raise our hands in class to ask for help or ask a question and some students in the class laugh or make fun of us. We become embarrassed, feel humiliated, and experience rejection. Some of us clam up and go through the rest of our lives afraid to ask for help because we fear rejection. Our prides are hurt. Our egos are fragile. We can easily be wounded. Therefore, we choose to go through life not knowing answers instead of seeking help.

I'm glad our son, Marcus, was not ashamed to ask for help. We discovered that he had a learning disability (learning difference). In the first and second grades we could tell that he was struggling with his studies. We discovered that he was dyslexic. Many of you may know what dyslexia means. For those who don't, it is when you sometimes see and read things backwards. For example, dyslexics may see the number 16 as 61, or the word *was* as *saw*.

In the early 80's, there was no school in our area – in fact, there was no school in America – that could address his learning disability. We had to enroll him in an alternative school so he could be tutored properly. To make things more challenging, he was diagnosed with Attention Deficit Disorder (ADD). With much encouragement, assistance and tutoring from his teachers, Marcus was never ashamed to ask for help. He graduated from high school in 1991. (Thank you, Marcus, for never being afraid to ask for help. And thank you for knowing that applied knowledge is power.)

## 2. Learn to take notes.

Many students perceive themselves to be so smart that when they are in class they fail to take notes. When they get home they discover they've forgotten 97% of what the teacher said. I tell students it's okay to take notes in the classroom. I encourage them not to be intimidated by their peers. I also remind them that as they go higher in education, more will be expected from them by their teachers and employers. I emphasize that if they need help to improve their note taking skill, they should ask a teacher, peer, mentor or parent.

## 3. Learn to follow instructions.

Did you know that about 20% of the errors we make on our homework assignments and exams is because we do not follow instructions? Whether you are going to bake a cake or build a computer, your success depends on how well you follow instructions. You wouldn't expect a cake to taste delicious if you used the wrong ingredients. You should not expect a computer to function accurately without its complete wiring and computer chips properly installed. So why should you expect to make 100 on an exam if you're ill prepared? The next time you take an exam, read each question twice and follow the instructions. Do this, and you will experience positive results.

### 4. Start or join a study group.

One of the major mistakes freshmen make during their first year of college is thinking they don't need anyone's help. They isolate themselves from everyone on campus. Then reality sets in and they experience a crisis. They have no one to turn to for advice, encouragement and help. The earlier you join or start a study group, the better. Look for individuals who have the right values, commonalities, objectives and willingness that support the group.

I'd like to share a personal experience about the effectiveness of teams. When our daughter, Chambray, was in the fifth grade, she was asked to take a proficiency test to determine her grade level. The proficiency results showed that she was three grade levels behind. At first we suspected she wasn't really trying. Then we discovered she had a learning disability (learning difference) which was called, in layman's terms, short term and long term memory stability. For example, she could study for an exam, enter the classroom and score 100% on a test. Then she could take the same exam two or three days later and her score would fall between zero and 10%. The problem was that she was learning the subject material at a superficial level, but it was not reaching the deep memory section of her brain.

We met with the principal and her teachers, then as a team, we developed a game plan which involved home tutoring and extra help at school to help bring Chambray up to her actual grade level.

By the end of the third year she was back on 8th grade level and ready for her freshman year in high school. Chambray was willing to help herself because she wanted to be a member of the Class of 2000. She made it! She graduated with her peers. We are so proud of her perseverance and hard work.

> **A Backpack Keeper:** Never get so much in a hurry that you don't learn something every day.

## Nobody's Perfect

You have no doubt heard the expression "nobody's perfect." And it's true, none of us is perfect. Our flaws are what cause so many lost opportunities. But our flaws are also our teachers. They force us to take stock of ourselves. They are also the very things that allow us to experience humility and empathy. These two qualities lead to an attitude of gratitude and forgiveness once we see our flaws as shortcomings and not life sentences.

Few things take a heavier toll on us than being led to believe that there is only one way to do certain things. Sometimes there's no one best way. Understanding this is part of growing up and stretching out.

I came across a cute, but telling story in Gregory Bateson's book, *Steps to an Ecology of Mind.* It involved a poignant conversation he'd had with his pre-teen daughter. I'll paraphrase it for you since it was a lengthy recollection:

> *One day his serious-minded daughter asked him a very interesting question: "Daddy, why does everything get muddled so easily?"*

*"What do you mean by 'muddled,' Sweet-heart?" he responded.*

*"Oh, you know," she said innocently. "It's when things don't go right. They're not perfect. Look at my dresser. My stuff is all over the place. None of it is in the right place. Everything's muddled."*

*"What do you mean, darling? Show me what you mean when everything is perfect.*

*She huffed impatiently.*

*"I'll show you." She moved everything that was "out of place" to its assigned position on her dresser.*

*"There. Now everything's perfect again."*

*Her father asked her, "What if I moved the photo Mom took of you over here?" He pointed to the opposite end of the dresser.*

*"No, Daddy. That would muddle everything."*

*"Suppose I moved your teddy bear from here to here," he teased, placing her favorite stuffed bear a few inches away from its original position.*

*"No, no, no. You're really making it muddled," she snapped, blocking the bear's three-inch migration.*

*"You mean if I move anything, I muddle every-thing?"*

*She nodded. Her father smiled and stooped so he was eye-level with his daughter.*

*"Sweetie, it's not so much that things get too muddled. It's that you've got too many ways for things to get muddled and only one way for things to be perfect."*

I believe people seek perfection because they are afraid to make mistakes or fail at something. For many people, the word *failure* carries with it a sense of finality, an air of fatalism, a hint of incompetence. It conjures up visions of diminished self-worth and loss of professional credibility. However, human error is inevitable – especially when something new and complex is being attempted. Crucifying someone for an honest mistake or failure leads to gun-shy decision-making and procrastination. On the other hand, keeping failure in perspective can be an empowering experience.

Some years ago, a promising IBM executive lost the company three million dollars in an ambitious, but risky, venture. High hopes turned into abysmal failure. An extraordinary business opportunity was lost. Thomas J. Watson, Sr. (IBM's founder) called the young executive into his office.

Before the Chief Executive could speak, the manager blurted out sincerely, "I'm truly sorry for causing you and the company so much grief. I intend to leave quietly. Here's my resignation."

"You can't be serious, young man," Watson replied. "We've just spent three million dollars educating you!"

What incredible vision! What extraordinary perceptiveness! I'm sure the young executive was surprised by his CEO's generosity. I'm also sure he didn't disappoint IBM's founder when he was given his next assignment. My point is, it's okay to fail. The important thing is to learn from your mistakes and don't make the same mistake twice. Now don't get me wrong. I'm not asking you to condone sloppiness, slipshod work, intentional carelessness or the like. I have zero tolerance for those kinds of mistakes. What I would like to urge you to do is to enthusiastically applaud honest attempts that go awry and look for ways to learn from mistakes. Look for the diamond in the rough. There's a lesson to be learned.

---

**Never see failure as failure, but
only as a learning experience.**

---

Oftentimes the fear of failure and rejection keeps us from reaching our goals, dreams, and success. Failure is okay. Know that there is no success without failure. In the previous chapter, we read twelve stories about different individuals that experienced both success and failure. In 1975 I learned valuable lessons from two of my mentors, J. Douglas Edwards and Tom Hopkins. They outlined what they called, "Attitudes Toward Failure."

1. **I never see failure as failure,** but only as a learning experience. Even though I learned this statement when I was 29 years old, I was reminded that the statement was given to me by my dad when I was nine years old. He gave me the exact same statement in Spanish. *Nunca mires un fracaso como un fracaso pero como una experiencia para aprender.*

   I had no clue what he was talking about 20 years ago. But when I learned the same phrase in English 20 years later from two mentors, I understood the impact of the words. It encouraged me to continue learning from all my experiences.

2. **I never see failure as failure,** but only as an opportunity to practice techniques which perfect my performance.

3. **I never see failure as failure,** but only as the negative feedback I need to change the course of my direction.

4. **I never see failure as failure,** but only as an opportunity to develop my sense of humor.

5. **I never see failure as failure,** but only as a game I must play to win.

Here is one I have added to this list:

6. **I never see failure as failure,** but only as an opportunity to forgive and love others.

> *I am not judged by the number of times I fail, but by the number of times I succeed, and the number of times I succeed is in direct proportion to the number of times I fail and keep on trying.*

I recommend you memorize all six attitudes toward failure. They have always helped me put things in the proper perspective. Even though I have shared these attitudes towards failure with my family, the first one is the one I have drilled into the minds of my children: Marcus, Alétta and Chambray.

One day several years ago I got home from work early. As I pulled into the driveway, I noticed my nine-year old son, Marcus, in the garage. He seemed pretty uptight about something. He was screaming and throwing tools against the walls of the garage.

"Marcus, what's up?" I said. "What's going on? Why this destructive behavior?"

He looked at me angrily. With tears in his eyes, he said, "Look Dad, I tore down my bike and cleaned all the parts and now when I try to put the bike back together, I end up with extra parts."

I tried my best not to smile as I listened to him patiently while he explained his predicament.

Then after a few moments, I said, "Ok, Marcus, let's slow down a little and evaluate your situation. First of all I want you to repeat the statement you've learned about failure."

No response from Marcus. "Come on Marcus, say it."

He looked at me again. Reluctantly he said, "I never see failure as failure, but only as a learning experience."

"Excellent. Now what is the lesson you learned here?"

"Well, Dad, I learned how not to put my bike together!"

"Good," I responded and then walked back into the house. Why did I walk away without helping him? Because I couldn't fix it. I didn't know anything about bicycles! About an hour later, I noticed he was riding his bike up and down the street. I am confident he saw failure as a learning experience that day. And I am just as sure he learned that he knew a lot more about bicycle repair than he thought he knew. I knew Marcus had the knowledge to assemble his bike. All he needed was the incentive to start over.

> *A major key to success is:*
> *when you fail, simply start over.*

Both success and failure are the results of cumulative choices. It's the poor choices each day that contribute to people's frustration and failure. Scores of thoughtless decisions over time lead to failure. Excuses to justify inaction and poor decision-making lead to failure and disillusionment. Bowing to expediency usually sabotages your success. However, thoughtful choices each day can also result in successful outcomes. Deciding to hold yourself to a higher standard leads to success. Unselfishly contributing to someone's welfare leads to success. Delaying personal gratification long enough to wait for good results generally leads to lasting success. Having the courage to make ethical decisions guarantees elevated feelings of self-worth and respect.

> **A Backpack Keeper:** Knowing has not, is not and will not ever be enough. Knowledge is a good start, but applying the *right* knowledge at the *right* time, under the *right* circumstances is the key to your success.

# People Will Pay You For What You Know

One of the things I love to do during an assembly is reward a student who answers one of my questions. My rationale is that there is a lesson to be learned and I will guarantee you that the recipient will not forget the lesson. I begin by making the statement: "People will pay you for what you know." Then I ask a question. One of my favorites is: "Who can name the last five presidents of the United States of America?"

As of this writing, in all the times I have done this exercise there have always been students who have given the correct answer. I make a big deal of it, asking the student to come forward. After offering my congratulations, I hand the

98

student a $20 bill for having the correct answer. I love to see the reaction on each student's face when I hand over twenty bucks. Where's the camera when you need one?

After the applause, I share the lesson they just learned. I tell them: "When I finish my presentation and leave this auditorium, if the only thing you remember is that I gave away some money, you should have never invited me. But I will guarantee you that the student who received the $20 bill will never forget that "people will pay you for what you know."

The students on the receiving end of my $20 handout are being rewarded for their specialized knowledge. Generalized knowledge would not have gotten them very far. They had to be familiar with a particular area of United States history or political science – the Presidency. They also had to have the initiative and the courage to stand before their peers and answer a question fired at them by someone who obviously had his own agenda and could have rewarded them or embarrassed them.

Each of these $20 winners exemplifies an important truth when it comes to acquiring knowledge. Most people believe knowledge is power, but knowledge is only potential power – and only certain types of knowledge transform that potential into usable ends. My point is you can have considerable knowledge – even specialized knowledge in a certain area – and still not be paid well for what you know. The secret to lasting success is you must make the right knowledge available at the right time, under the right circumstances to the right people. Follow that simple backpack rule and you'll enjoy phenomenal success.

I am sure you have seen data showing the average income earnings in America. As of this writing, the average figures on the annual income people make compared go their level of education paint a compelling picture:

| Income By Degree | |
| --- | --- |
| **Type of Degree** | **Average Income Per Year** |
| No High School Diploma | $12,000 - $15,000 |
| High School Diploma | $16,000 -$ 23,000 |
| Some College or Trade School | $22,000 - $29,000 |
| Undergraduate Degree | $27,000 - $37,000 |
| Masters Degree | $37,000 - $45,000 |
| Doctorate | $45,000 - $75,000 |
| Specialized Degree | $90,000 - $180,000 |

Opportunities are there for all of us. Fall in love with learning and apply what you learn. Inventory the contents of your backpack. Make sure you pack plenty of specialized knowledge into it. Start wherever you are to add to your knowledge base. If you've dropped out of school, get back in or take the high school equivalency exam. If you've stopped reading, start reading again. If you stopped your formal education at the high school level, go to college, technical school or become certified in a speciality area. Whatever you do, don't stop learning, because learning is earning.

> **A Backpack Keeper:** There is no such thing as a success ceiling.

# Lengthen Your Learning Curve

As a Hispanic, I am concerned about the drop out rate of Hispanic students from high school and college. To understand how the percentages fall, suppose 100 Hispanic children enroll in Kindergarten. Of these 100 kids, only 50 will graduate from high school. Then, of the 50, only 10 will enroll into college. Of that 10, only one will graduate from college. I am sure that other groups have similar stories. We must change this now! We must see what we can do to ensure that 100% of students who start high school graduate. Then we must encourage every student to attend college, technical school, trade school or the military. By accomplishing this mandate, we will have skilled and trained individuals in our future labor force to keep America competitive in the global marketplace.

To illustrate the power of an individual's influence on a young person's choice about school, I'd like to tell you about a life-changing encounter I had with my older brother, Raymond, when I was a youngster. Although he had dropped out of school, he always had plenty of money, a car, girls and cool friends. He was my hero. I wanted to be just like him—tough, muscular and menacing. I suppose he would be called a gang leader today. He could have played the key male roles in both the West-Side Story and Grease.

His skills in defending himself with a knife were phenomenal. He could leap in the air from a standing position, and kick and cut an opponent at the same time. He could have given the karate king, Bruce Lee, a run for his money.

On one particular occasion, I asked him to teach me to be like him. I remember the steel in his eyes and the intensity of his gaze before he spoke.

"Are you sure you want to be just like me?" he countered. The smile which creased his lips was the smile of a young man wise beyond his years, a man who had graduated summa cum laude from the school of hard knocks.

I nodded my head. He took out his knife and demonstrated his exquisite knife-handling skills. I was awe struck. Before I knew it he lunged toward me in a lightning-fast move and placed his knife at my forehead. He had negotiated over six feet of distance in the blink of an eye. I froze, too surprised to speak and too frightened to move.

"Little brother," he said in a carefully controlled voice, "if you ever get a tattoo of a cross on your hands or forehead, or anywhere else for that matter. I will cut the tattoo out." The same surprise that leaped onto my face flung my mouth open.

"And if you ever drop out of school," he continued, "I will bury you. You will not be like me, nor will you drop out of school. Do you understand me?"

I smothered a small gasp before I spoke.

"Okay. Okay." I whispered, trying to stand on legs that felt like spaghetti.

Sensing my alarm, Raymond knelt in front of me and clasped my head in his strong hands. His wise smile was a hymn. Then he stood and tousled my hair. "Let's go inside," he said as he lovingly placed his hand on my shoulder.

If you'll take a quick peek at my photo on the back jacket of this book, you'll notice I have no tattoos – and I finished school. I have shared this story because I believe that sometimes someone has to put the fear of God in us to wake us up. In my case it was my older brother, whom I still very much admire, trust and love. He was there at a point in my life when I needed guidance and direction. He left his mark on me. It is my sincere hope that something I say in this book will leave its mark on you so you can become the kind of person you were meant to be.

If you're looking for the right career, job or future, look in the right places. Packing your backpack with the right skills and education will open the right doors and keep you on the right path. My brother, Mike, gave me a great analogy for staying on the right path. A few years ago, Mike attended his 30th class reunion. As he entered the room holding the reunion festivities, he was greeted by one of his classmates and ushered to his table. When he got to the table, ten of his classmates were sharing short reviews of their lives, families and successes. Then one of his classmates made a startling remark. "You know, Mike, back in high school you and your family made it in spite of the odds. You were one of the few Hispanics who went to college and earned your Masters degree. We applaud your accomplishments."

Mike responded by saying, "Let me make an observation. I know that all of you went to college. I'll bet your conversations at the dinner table all through school were probably centered around life after high school, and the colleges you would attend. Am I right?"

They all agreed.

Mike continued, "In our family, our focus was to make sure we at least finished high school and secured a good job. My mom and dad only went to the first and second grade, so if three sons finished high school, that would have been a milestone for our family. There is a reason why my brothers and I went to college. We talked about college the same as you did. We talked about what we were going to do with our lives in elementary school. We had few Hispanic role models. But we had made up our minds in the fourth or fifth grade that we were going to finish high school and go to college. Now, with our children, our discussions are not only whether they will attend college, but which college they will attend."

I mention both Raymond's and Mike's stories because I believe our decision to continue our education is made long before the actual day we enroll in our first college course. I believe children make up their minds whether or not to finish high school in the fourth or fifth grade. I tell my school audiences to think beyond elementary, middle and high school, and to add lifelong education to their backpacks so they will be prepared for the business realities of the 21st Century.

> **A Backpack Keeper:** If you can't be a
> Rhodes Scholar,
> be a Roads Scholar –
> master the school of hard knocks.

# Make Wise Decisions

In her terrific book, *Tongue Fu*, Sam Horn said her goal was to "develop real-life responses that people could use immediately to handle the challenges they face on a daily basis." She called these *zinger* responses *tongue fu*. Well, I have developed what I call *Decision Karate*. The following ten decision-making rules will help you make better decisions:

1. **Accept the fact that you will make mistakes.** Every decision is a risk, meaning that you may experience some failure. What's worse than a bad decision is the agony of not making a decision at all. Not making a decision is a decision in and of itself. A rule of thumb: if you are not failing occasionally, you are not taking enough risks. So, when you make a mistake, view it as a learning experience. When you fail, just start over.

2. **Remember you can always change your mind.** Decisions are not only adjustable, but also revocable. Relax. You can't know everything. Don't sacrifice your credibility by refusing to change an ill-advised decision. Modify it or adjust it. Take decisive corrective measures. Knowing when to cut your losses is a great *backpack* skill to have.

3. **Don't fall into the trap that says: "I'll wait until I gather all the facts."** Let me introduce a new phrase to some of you – Paralysis of Analysis. This is where we never feel we have enough facts to make a wise decision, so we continue searching for additional information beyond what is reasonable. In our lives and careers, we almost never have enough information to make a decision we know will be 100% accurate. I am not suggesting that you forget gathering facts and data, but realize you may not always have the luxury of waiting 'til that moment of absolute certainty arrives. Therefore, the decision must be made with the information at hand. Don't get hung up on the impossible task of trying to gather all the facts prior to making a decision.

4. **Break your routine and usual thought patterns.** As human beings, we love routine, familiarity and being comfortable with certain patterns in our lives. Content in our way of life, we don't want to rock the boat – in other words, if it ain't broke, don't fix it. The only definition our mind knows is what we tell it, which is referred to as conditioning our mind. We tend to go with the tried and true instead of creating new solutions. Sometimes a change of scenery is all that is needed to snap you into a more decisive and creative mode. For example, try taking a different route home; sitting at a different spot at lunchtime; or taking a walk for the purpose of contemplating a major decision.

5. **Respect your intuition.** Remember all those hunches (gut feelings) you never acted upon? We have all missed intuitive opportunities. I urge you to take your hunches seriously. More and more people are discovering that hunches are not just random

emotional feelings. They are the result of accessing the vast knowledge and experiences in our subconscious mind. When something looks right, but feels wrong – or vice versa – it can be a sign to pause and pay close attention. Keep a mental record of these feelings and you will develop a *consciousness of confidence* to respond correctly to your intuitive instincts.

**6. Do not be afraid of seeking the opinion of others.** Never be ashamed to ask for help. Ask friends, peers, co-workers, bosses, parents, relatives, counselors, business coaches, teachers, and other credible people for their advice. This process is not...I repeat...is not to be used to change your decision but to reaffirm your decision. If you ask the opinion of others, be careful not to telegraph your own opinion about the decision. In other words, state your situation, then listen respectfully to their opinion. Remember, you have the final responsibility for every decision you make.

**7. Seek the advice of an expert.** Our decisions come in various degrees of priority, complexity and seriousness, so do not rush important decisions. Call or visit a mentor, spiritual advisor or authoritative figure you highly respect. This individual can give you the right information you need to make a decision. This process may take more time, but it should help minimize your risk.

**8. Conduct a quick analysis of the decision options.** Relax! This is not as difficult as it sounds. Write the decision options on a piece of paper, then ask the following questions about each option you are considering: What is my level of control? What are the implications of this decision? Who will be affected?

What is the level of risk? What is the probability of success? Do I have the resources I need to implement it? Weigh each option against the others, using these questions, to identify the option best suited for you at this time.

9.  **Let someone else decide.** You cannot delegate the ultimate responsibility for your decision-making. But in many situations, you can delegate most of the work that leads to the decision. For example, suppose you want to compare two computers that appear to be equal in quality, options and price. You feel an urgency to decide, but you do not have the time to make the comparisons. Delegate the job to someone who is familiar with the technologies and who is also a person you can trust. Then review the comparison data and make the right decision. The ownership of the original decision was never transferred…it was supported.

10. **Use the Good – Better – Best Model.**

Good = I know.

Better = I know that I know.

Best = I know that I know that I know.

It's always good to take a step back and evaluate your feelings about your decisions. How certain are you that you have made the right decision? One of the best barometers I know is the Good – Better – Best Model. Basically, it works this way. I know I've made the best possible decision when I move up the scale from good to better to best. It's a simple, but effective evaluation. Try it the next time you have to make an important decision. You'll find that it's an invaluable barometer for successful decision-making.

# Backpack Wisdom

1. The more we learn, the more we realize how little we actually know.

2. Be good at something that brings joy and helps people.

3. No acquired knowledge is wasted unless it isn't applied.

4. Our flaws are only shortcomings, not life sentences.

5. See failures as learning experiences because there is no success without failure at some point along the way.

6. Applying the right knowledge at the right time, under the right circumstances to the right people is the key to lasting success.

# People Skills Help Ensure Your Success

# Chapter 5

# People Skills Help Ensure Your Success

*You can get everything in life you want if you will just help enough other people get what they want.* (Zig Ziglar)

Back in high school there was this guy who was one of the most popular individuals on campus and around town. He had a very expressive personality. He was happy-go-lucky, a ladies' man, arrogant and a show-off. He had the reputation of being the life of the party and usually got anything he wanted, including any girl he wanted.

I remember one day he wanted to date a young Hispanic girl. He was well aware of the Hispanic tradition which required young men who wanted to date young Hispanic women to ask the permission of her parents. Reluctantly this guy made the appointment to see her parents. He knew this was only a formality and he was confident there would be no problem securing his date. After an hour of good old-fashioned grilling, the father asked the young man what he wanted with his daughter. He told her father he wanted to date his daughter. So the father called his daughter into the room to witness his decision.

The father flatly refused the young man's request and forbid his daughter to ever date this guy. When the surprised young man asked her father why he couldn't take his daughter out, the father told him it was because of his reputation. The girl's father explained that he was nothing but a show-off and that he disrespected the girls he dated.

He told the shocked young man, "You treat young women as less than human beings, and all you want is to put another notch on your belt. My beautiful daughter will never be a notch on anyone's belt."

So much can be said about how you present yourself to others. Be aware of your appearance. Pay attention to the neatness and cleanliness of your clothing. Personal hygiene plays a major role in how people respond to you, too. When you present yourself to others, be present in mind and body. Wherever you go, you take your physical appearance and mental attitude with you. People make decisions about the kind of person you are: your skills, attitudes, values and beliefs; and your potential as a friend, work associate or, as in the case above, whether or not you will date a certain young woman.

> **A Backpack Keeper:** People judge you on how you present yourself verbally, vocally and visually.

# First Impressions are Lasting Impressions

I believe most of us realize how crucial first impressions can be. We try to "get off to a good start" when we meet people by presenting ourselves in the best possible light. We attempt to conceal our short-comings and "put our best foot forward." One of the most over-used expressions when it comes to meeting people for the first time is still so much on target that I'm going to repeat it here: "You never get a second chance to make a first impression." This statement always has been and always will be true when it comes to interpersonal relationships. For example, suppose I asked you to describe someone who is characterized by the following adjectives: intelligent, industrious, good-looking, stubborn, impulsive and moody. Jot down your impression of that individual. Now I want you to describe the following person: Moody, impulsive, stubborn, good-looking, industrious, intelligent.

The only difference in the two perceptions is the order in which the adjectives appeared. The first list began with the word *intelligent*. It initially described the person in positive terms. The second list of adjectives began with the word *moody*, which, of course, is viewed as being a negative attribute. First impressions set the stage for the personal encounters which follow. They create the tone for conversations and affect the way people decide to interact with you.

> *You never get a second chance to make a first impression.*

A lesson to all of us has been around since the beginning of time. You may be familiar with the old adage "first impressions are lasting impressions." In people skills, remember the 7/11 rule. The rule is that within 7 seconds of meeting another person, 11 impressions are made of you in the mind of the other person. These impressions come from both conscious and sub-conscious levels. People decide if you are knowledgeable, if you are a good listener, if you are honest and dependable, whether you are credible, if you seem responsible, if you are friendly and sociable, whether you are being attentive and helpful, and so on.

My point is that almost all of the messages we send people during those 7 initial seconds determine their opinion of us. It is not so much what we say, but how we look and act when we say it. It's in our gestures, our tone of voice, our appearance and our attitudes. Their assessment of our worth and credibility is also affected by our facial expressions, our posture, the physical distance between us and the person to whom we are speaking, and the way we make eye contact.

> *Wherever you go, whatever you do, you take your body and attitudes with you.*

When you greet others, make a conscious effort to make direct eye contact. I have found that less than 10% of individuals make direct eye contact when they greet others. Here's a technique I teach to make sure people make eye contact. It is simple to use and easy to master, but it does take practice. The next time you introduce yourself to another person, make sure you look directly into that person's eyes without staring. When you walk away, ask yourself, "What color were his or her eyes?" If you can immediately remember the color of their eyes, you made direct eye contact. By maintaining direct eye contact, you show your respect for the other person. They will see you as a confident person and want you more involved in their life or business.

In addition to the 7/11 rule, I'd like to introduce you to the 10-foot rule. When you come within 10 feet of another person, make eye contact and acknowledge that person's presence. The reason this is so important is because people can *hear* where you are *looking*. One of my favorite stories about the importance of eye contact is the one about the first time the great American artist, Norman Rockwell, met General Eisenhower:

> *(We) didn't discuss politics or the campaign. Mostly we talked about painting and fishing. But what I remember most about the one and a half hours I spent with him was the way he gave me his full attention. He never took his eyes off me. He listened to me and talked to me as if he didn't have anything else to do. You'd never know he was on the brink of a presidential campaign.*

How many times have you talked to someone who broke eye contact with you to see who else was in the room? Has someone ever glanced away in response to some kind of distraction, indicating that you did not have their full time and attention? Have you ever been to a meeting or luncheon where the person talking to you rarely made eye contact or spoke directly to you? I can tell you, not receiving the eye contact you think you deserve is frustrating.

Because eye contact is such a fundamental people skill, I call eye CONTACT an eye CONTRACT! And like any other contract, it needs to be signed, sealed and delivered.

When someone diverts his or her gaze inappropriately during face-to-face discussions, he or she has just broken one of the most fundamental "contracts" in human relations. As a keynote speaker, I work very hard to keep that "eye contract" with my audiences. I want each member of my audience, whether I speak to 500 or 5,000, to feel that I'm speaking to him or her individually.

> **Wandering eyes can cause permanent damage to any relationship – business or otherwise.**

Eyes speak volumes. A person who has wide eyes is considered to be personable, frank, outgoing, fun-loving, and even naive. People who look down a lot are seen as shy, modest, subdued or unsure of themselves.

Stares are associated with rudeness, arrogance, coldness or outright hostility. When people roll their eyes, they are usually communicating amusement, criticism, disinterest or fatigue. As you can see, the eyes reveal a lot about us. And they are especially telling during first impressions.

Here are some "eye care" tips for managing first impressions:

- Maintain direct eye contact without staring.
- Avoid excessive blinking or squinting.
- Refrain from letting your eyes wander.
- Avoid rolling your eyes.
- Refrain from rubbing or scratching your eyes.

Your eye behavior isn't the only thing that affects how people judge you during first impressions. The way you dress and your over-all appearance also dictate how they feel about you. Your physical appearance is your visual resumé. It is part of your over-all communication package. You strike a certain image by the way you walk, dress and appear to others. If you want your first impressions to be positive, you must assume conscious control over the way you look.

One of the first things I notice about people is the way they look, how they carry themselves, what kind of posture they have, their personal grooming and the style of clothing they wear. I have discovered that dressing properly may not get you the job, the promotion or the date – but dressing inappropriately can definitely remove you from consideration.

> *Your physical appearance is your visual resumé.*

Have you ever noticed that when you look good, you feel good? And when you feel good, you look good to others. I believe clothing is the extension of our personalities. All of us have different tastes in clothing. Some of us dress conservatively. Others are more liberal, and even bizarre, in their tastes. Men wearing Rolex watches and women adorned in Ralph Lauren ensembles are considered wealthy. A student wearing glasses and carrying a laptop computer is perceived as intelligent. A young woman dressed in an official Olympic jersey is admired for her athleticism. While we can't always "tell a book by its cover," we make assumptions about its contents.

Your "visual resumé," like your career resumé, must pass scrutiny. Otherwise, people will form negative opinions of you based on their initial impressions. That may seem unfair, but it's true. When you're in the public eye, you can't afford to have a "bad hair day." A wrinkled shirt or blouse, dirty fingernails, scuffed footwear and unkempt facial hair can turn first impressions into visual depressions, losing you valued opportunities because of the way you look.

> **A Backpack Keeper:** Impression management is another way of saying people management.

# Protect Your Reputation

Reputation is very critical for your success and making your mark in this world. Your reputation is what you are. Your reputation is also how you want others to perceive you. In the story I used to open this chapter, the tainted reputation of the brash, young man preceded him. On campus as a student or on the job as an employee, build a strong reputation and protect it. People pay attention to your reputation. I guarantee you they will talk about you to others. By building a strong positive reputation you won't ever have to worry about defending your good name. There is an old adage, "walk your talk and talk your walk."

A lesson I learned from Jim Rohn in 1978 about the importance of protecting your reputation made a lasting impression on me. He said, "Be who you say you are or quit saying who you are." If I say that I am a good student, then I will be a good student or keep my mouth shut. If I say I am a good parent, then I'd best be a good parent or keep my mouth shut.

His words continue to haunt me and quite frankly, I hope they haunt you as well. Please don't take this statement as a negative reminder or see it as a guilt trip. Use it to remind yourself that your reputation is critical for your success.

---

> **Be who you say you are,
> or quit saying who you are.**

One of the first things you can do to build a solid base of positive people skills is to acknowledge the importance of respecting yourself and others. Much of that respect has to do with your personal credibility, and the value of your good name. For example, the name Cabrera is well-respected in our community. Cabreras are known for their hard work, pride, penchant for responsibility, fairness, ethics, caring and integrity. As a child, I had a lot to live up to. Growing up I realized that I had to acknowledge and protect the reputation of my family's good name.

What is your word worth? How much value do you place on your word? When you give your word, do you keep it? Do you mean what you say or is it just lip service? When people recognize that your word is your bond, they will go out of their way to do business with you and support you in every way. I can remember when a bank loaned my dad $15,000 for a home loan on a hand shake. Wow, just on a hand shake! I wonder how often we see that in today's world. My dad's honorable reputation preceded him. I grew up being proud of the name Cabrera, and I do everything within my power to honor my dad by making sure my good name precedes me, too!

As we follow the news today, we see how America is being affected by all the corporate scandals. From moral decay to business corruption, the value of some people's word has taken a major downward shift. So make sure your word remains your bond, your strength and your testimony.

**118**

You will not only be attracted to success, but success will be attracted to you.

> ## A Backpack Keeper: Your word is your bond.

## *Increase Your Ear-Ability*

Good listening is everyone's business. That's about as succinctly as I can put it. Bill Gates puts it this way: *"When words fail, listening comes in very handy."* And yet, it is one of the least developed of our people skills. I often repeat the well-known expression: *God gave us two ears and one mouth, that should tell us something.* I've stated the obvious, of course, but true *backpack* people know how important listening is to their success in both business and in life.

When we listen, we can hear the world around us in magical ways. The following well-known story illustrates the power of attentive listening:

> *A man and woman were strolling along a crowded sidewalk in a downtown business area. Suddenly one of them exclaimed, "Did you hear that bark?*
>
> *They both stopped and listened intently. "There it is again. Didn't you hear it?" asked the one who heard the puppy a second time.*
>
> *"How can you hear that puppy's bark in this frenzied city?"*
>
> *The companion, who was a veterinarian-turned-animal rights advocate, smiled but did not explain. She simply took a quarter out of her purse*

*and dropped it on the sidewalk, causing a dozen
people to look around for the loose change.*

"We hear," she said, "what we expect to hear."

We hear hundreds of sounds each minute, but we listen
to only a few sounds, the sounds we view as meaningful and
relevant to our safety, health, interests and well-being.

We block out the other sounds. As in the story I just
shared, we choose to hear what we expect to hear. New students in school and new employees at work may be
bothered by all of the noise until they become familiar with
the hustle and bustle. People who live in the suburbs grow
accustomed to the sound of crickets and the chorus of birds,
while city folk become fascinated by the symphony of natural sounds. In both cases, people notice unfamiliar sounds
and ignore familiar, commonplace sounds.

Let's take a closer look at the distinction between listening and hearing. According to *Webster's New World
Collegiate Dictionary*, listening is the "ability to make a
conscious, purposeful effort to hear" or "to pay attention to
what is heard." Hearing, on the other hand, is the "sense by
which sound is perceived by the ear." Hearing involves the
physiological reception of sound, while listening involves
the perception of meaningful sound. Listening, then, is a
choice. It is the voluntary emotional response to the sounds
we choose to listen to, out of all the sounds we are capable
of hearing.

Since listening is a choice, you can become a better listener if you want to become a better listener. And you will
become a better listener when you practice listening. And
practice you must, because like any other skill, listening
takes commitment. There are a number of reasons why people's "ear-ability" is not as developed as their other abilities.
People generally speak at the rate of 140 to 190 words per
minute. We listen at 350 to 500 words per minute. So people spend the "extra" processing time going on mental

vacations, daydreaming or thinking about what they are going to say next.

People are usually "listening challenged" when they are OUTCLASSED:

Ordered or directed sternly to do something.

Unduly criticized, blamed, shamed or embarrassed.

Told what they should or should not do.

Cursed at or called a demeaning name.

Lectured at unmercifully.

Angry and upset.

Sure they don't need help.

Severely questioned or ridiculed.

Enthusiastically telling their story.

Disagreed with by someone they dislike.

You will be able to win friends and influence a lot of people if you adopt the following listening habits:

1. **Say people's names correctly.** A person's name is, to that person, the sweetest, most important sound in any language.

2. **Listen attentively.** Give the person you are listening to your full time and attention.

3. **Block out competing thoughts and sounds.** Remember, your ears work twice as fast as your mind works and five times as fast as the average person speaks. So, fight the temptation to wander off.

4. **Don't interrupt people.** Give people a chance to finish their sentence. People hate to be interrupted.

5. **Listen with your whole body.** Maintain appropriate eye contact, lean slightly forward to show interest, nod your head occasionally, listen face-to-face.

6. **Listen between the lines.** Sometimes the most important thing is what's *not* said.

7. **Ask clarifying questions.** Hold your questions until the other person can handle the interruption. Timing is everything.

8. **Take notes, but don't over-do notetaking.** Don't hesitate to pull out a note pad or palm pilot to capture important information. Be economical in your notetaking so you don't distract the speaker.

9. **Don't fake listening.** Don't let your inattention "leak" into your facial expressions and nonverbal body language. If you are unable to listen fully, reschedule the meeting or discussion for a time that is more convenient.

10. **Avoid mercenary listening.** Refrain from calling attention to mispronounced words, criticizing someone's accent or dialect and intentionally trying to trip someone up or confuse them.

Can you name someone who is a good listener, someone who really, really listens? What makes that person a great listener? I'm going to guess that out of all the people you know, you may be able to think of only one or two who qualify as great listeners. How do you feel when you are on the receiving end of a good listener? One of the most important gifts you can give someone during a conversation is to listen so attentively that that person has the impression he/she is the most important person in your world at the moment. For some people, conversation is a competitive exercise in which the first person to draw a breath is declared the listener. Most people don't listen, they just hang around impatiently for their turn to talk. Putting your thoughts on hold long enough to give someone your full time and attention is a skill that will help you win friends and influence people.

Active listening involves what I call the *3 L Formula.* Quite simply, it helps you put feeling into your listening by:

**Looking –** Look directly at the person who is speaking. Give him or her your undivided attention. Refrain from looking at other people nearby or glancing around the room. Avoid things like looking at your watch, brushing lint off your sleeve, playing with your hair, and so on. Avoiding these behaviors tells the other person that he or she has your undivided attention.

**Lifting –** Lifting your eyebrows occasionally shows interest and awareness. It lets the person know you are paying attention and that you are actively involved in the discussion.

**Leaning –** Part of good conversational etiquette is leaning forward to show your interest in what the other person is saying. This "edge-of-the-seat" interest confirms your attentiveness and communicates the fact that you are "there" for the other person.

In his funny book, *Down Time*, Ron Dentinger quips, "My wife used to talk to herself…she thought I was listening." Dentinger was kidding, of course, because people *do* know when you are not listening. The 3 L's generally let people know you are listening. People can sense when the person to whom they are speaking is distracted.

I am reminded of how important engaged listening is whenever I have the opportunity to speak to school children. I can say this with absolute confidence – if you want children to know you are really listening to them, kneel or sit down so you can speak eye-to-eye. Children (and most adults for that matter) are reluctant to open themselves up to someone who towers over them. Unless you are literally, and figuratively, on their level, youngsters will be hesitant to share their true feelings.

The same thing applies to adults. If you aren't on someone's level emotionally, philosophically, ethically or morally, their level of self-disclosure and openness will be affected.

> **A Backpack Keeper:** Put your ears in gear before you put your mouth in motion.

# Building Winning Relationships

Rewarding relationships are based on one of the oldest and most enduring rules of human interaction: *Do unto others as you would have them do unto you.* This maxim remains now, as it has since the beginning of time, one of the cardinal rules – if not the ultimate rule – of human relations. It is the basis of all of our moral and ethical social contracts. If you look deeply at any healthy family, community, society or nation, you will find that unifying thread in action. The relationship they form is a product of interdependence, trust, love and respect – which are the chief ingredients in building winning relationships.

One of the amazing things about human relationships is that people mimic what they see and repeat what they hear. That's why it's so important to act in positive, life-affirming ways. People will follow your lead. They will mimic your behavior. So it's important to model the same behavior you expect in others. Your ability to get along with other people is an indication of who you are and how you feel about yourself. You have to *be* the kind of person you want to be around – and that means appreciate your unique talents and abilities.

> **People mimic what they see
> and repeat what they hear.**

The following story, originally published in *The Book of Modern-Day Parables* by Fulton Oursler, illustrates the importance of *doing unto others as you would have them do unto you:*

> *A young woman living in New York's upscale Central Park South district had more money than she could possibly spend and everything she had ever wished for – except for one thing, a healthy child. Her beautiful five-year-old daughter was deathly ill and no one knew what to do. New York's finest doctors were at a loss as to the nature of her daughter's illness. She had spared no expense in her attempts to save her daughter's life. She was about to give up hope when she read in The New York Times of a world-renowned doctor from Switzerland who was coming to New York to lecture at NYU's prestigious School of Medicine.*
>
> *The mother instinctively knew that this world-famous disease specialist was the one who could save her child. She called her family physicians and several of the other specialists who were familiar with her predicament and asked them to use their influence to help her get an appointment with him. She used her own status and position to call, write and plead for his assistance – to no avail. Then one rainy afternoon, during one of her*

*crying spells, a short, portly, bearded man knocked
on her door. He was drenched from head-to-toe.*

*"What do you want?" she hissed.*

*"I beg your pardon, ma'am," he began, "but I
seem to have lost my way and wonder if I could use
your phone to call my driver. Do you mind?"*

*"Well, I'm sorry,' she replied sternly, "I have a
very sick daughter and do not want her to be dis-
turbed. I only opened the door to stop you from
knocking."*

*She waved him off the threshold and closed
the door.*

*Later that evening, a TV news story about the
Swiss doctor caught her attention. When she got a
glimpse of the doctor on the news channel, she discovered it was the same man she had closed the
door on that morning. She collapsed on the sofa,
realizing she had refused to help the man who
could have saved her daughter.*

You would be surprised how many times this story is
repeated each day, as people close the door on fantastic
opportunities when opportunity knocks. Winning relationships cannot be built on toxins such as rudeness, selfishness,
dishonesty and deceit. Negative attitudes and behaviors like
these cause relationship erosion. They destroy the founda-
tions of friendship and make healthy relationships difficult
to begin or maintain.

What can you do as an individual to build winning relationships? I have already discussed the importance of first
impressions, eye contact, listening and protecting your good
name. What follows are 15 people skills that lead to supe-
rior relationships and solid friendships. You will find them
to be invaluable communication tools to help you win

friends, influence people positively and gain an incredible competitive edge in school, business and life.

# Fifteen Incredible People Skills

1. **Remember people's names.** You've heard this a thousand times, but it's still at the top of the people skills list.

2. **Be generous in your praise and stingy in your criticism.** No one likes to be criticized – whether the criticism is "constructive" or not. Whenever you offer "constructive" advice, make sure you criticize the behavior and not the person.

3. **Be respectful of others.** Accept people for who they are. Show people you are sensitive to their needs.

4. **Show your sense of humor.** Most people take life much too seriously. Humor takes the edge off of stress and tension. It is an excellent coping strategy.

5. **Learn how to smile and laugh – often.** Smiles elevate your immune system, and so do grins. Laughter is medicinal. It is the chief medicine of the weary.

6. **Become a face in your community..** Volunteerism is one of the best training grounds for developing a healthy respect and appreciation for diversity.

> *People don't care how much you know until they know how much you care.*

7. **Handle conflict wisely.** Conflict occurs when two or more people attempt to occupy the same space (physically or ideologically) at the same time. Conflict is inevitable, natural and *manageable*. Learn how to use diplomacy, patience and foresight when push comes to shove.

8. **Expect the best in people.** People get what they expect to get. Expect the worst, you'll get the worst. Expect mediocrity, you'll get mediocrity. Expect the best, you'll get the best.

9. **Walk your talk.** Authenticity and credibility are absolutely necessary if you want to gain the loyalty and respect of others. People respect people they can trust and depend on.

10. **Give people the benefit of the doubt.** Positive expectations usually create self-fulfilling outcomes. Trust people until they give you a reason not to.

11. **Be empathetic.** People don't care how much you know until they know how much you care.

12. **Welcome new ideas.** Be open to the ideas and insights of others, because none of us is as smart as all of us.

> *People tend to repeat behavior*
> *they are rewarded for.*

13. **Be able to forgive.** Forgiveness is something you do for yourself. It is an emotional healing salve which allows you to move beyond the past and embrace the future.

128

**14. Become a diplomacy guru.** The art of negotiation and diplomacy turns foes into friends and conflicts into celebrations. Anyone can be polite to someone who is nice, but it takes a true diplomat to be polite to someone who is rude, demanding and arrogant.

**15. Know how to motivate people.** Realize that people tend to repeat behavior they are rewarded for, so be careful what you reward.

Developing these kinds of people skills is no easy task. It'll take hard work on your part – and plenty of patience. But develop them you must, because both your short-term and long-term success depend on how well you can build winning relationships. Each of these skills could be the subject of an entire book. I mention them here so you can begin filling your *backpack* with information about each one of them. Add them to your people skills repertoire. There's no telling how far you can go if you're willing to help enough people fill their backpacks with the principles you've learned in this book.

---

**A Backpack Keeper:** You can make more friends in a week by showing genuine interest in them than you can in a year by forcing them to get interested in you.

---

# Backpack Wisdom

1. People judge you on how you present yourself – verbally, vocally and visually.

2. You never get a second chance to make a first impression.

3. Your values, attitudes, beliefs and intentions go with you wherever you go.

4. Eye contact is an eye contract, so make sure you honor your "eye care" commitments.

5. Your physical appearance is your visual resumé.

6. Your word is your bond.

7. Model the same behavior you expect from others.

A

C

lways Set Realistic Goals

C

K

# Chapter 6

# Always Set Realistic Goals

*Become a mastermind with a master plan...Set goals...based on your desire...to succeed.* (Napoleon Hill)

We've covered a considerable amount of material in the first five chapters, most of which you can put to immediate use. This chapter is no exception. We've worked hard together to get you in a position to put the right things in your backpack. This chapter and the two which follow will add three more critical ingredients that will help guarantee your success in life.

The theme of this chapter is becoming a "goalmaker;" however, it will be quite different from any reading you have ever done on the subject of goals. The difference lies in this fact: goals are verbs and not nouns. Before you think I've just awakened from a long siesta, I want you to know that I'm absolutely serious about the verb vs. noun idea. The reason goals are verbs is because they are tactical means to strategic ends. Goals are the planned steps we take to turn the invisible into the visible.

What is a goal? *Webster's New World Collegiate Dictionary* states; 1. the line or place at which a race, trip, etc., is ended; 2. an object or end that one strives to attain, aim; 3. the act of scoring; 4, the score made.

To me the definition calls for intent and a plan of action. What do you want out of life, school, career, family? What do you want to accomplish during your lifetime?

Someone once said that *people who fail to plan, plan to fail.* You may want to read that italicized phrase again. Unfortunately that's where most people are – they simply fail to set clear, concise goals. Too many people struggle to make a living instead of designing a livelihood. They react to circumstances rather than plan their reactions. They believe goals are nouns, which means they see goals as outcomes instead of opportunities.

> ***People who fail to plan, plan to fail.***

Take a quick look around. What do you see? Are you sitting on a chair, the sofa, the floor or are you curled up in bed near the night light? Are you in your office? Are you surrounded by technology: a telephone, computer, laser printer, fax machine? Are you using a pen or marker to highlight or underline meaningful passages in this book? All of these items were once just ideas in someone's mind before they became material objects. They were technological outcomes that were the result of the imagination, planning, resourcefulness and practical applications, techniques of designers and engineers who created something from nothing. That's what *backpack* people do – create something from nothing. But that "nothing" starts with a deliberate, purposeful process called "Goalmaking."

> **A Backpack Keeper:** Our problem does not lie in setting our goals too high and missing; our problem lies in setting our goals too low and hitting.

## Become a "Goalmaker"

In the late 70's, I attended my first goal-setting workshop. I don't recall the name of the speaker or the workshop, but the results of his findings stuck. He shared the following results from a survey taken on setting goals. A group of 10,000 people were asked to describe in detail how they approached the goal-setting process. The results were as follows:

1. 3% of the 10,000 said they WROTE their goals down.

2. 17% said they THOUGHT about setting goals, but neglected to write them down or organize their thoughts.

3. 60% said they just LIVE week to week.
   - For adults who worked, that meant their goal was to work Monday through Friday and put in their 40 hours.
   - For students in school it meant that their goal was to weather a week's worth of school.

134

They couldn't wait to hear the last bell for dismissal on Friday.

4.  20% said that they just live for the end of each day's work or school.

    - Working adults just wanted to make it through the work day and check out at 5p.m.
    - Students refused to think beyond the last period of the day.

These are sobering statistics. However, the one that caused me to become a "goalmaker" was this one: the 3% of the 10,000 who WROTE their goals down became 50-to-70% more successful than their goal-deficient peers. I'm going to toss another statistic at you – the percentages haven't changed appreciably over the past 30 years. One thing is for certain, when you just live *week*-to-*week*, you become *weak*.

Some people believe it is the lot they draw in life and that there is nothing they can do about it. They make sure their negative self-fulfilling prophesy comes true. *Backpack* people, on the other hand, know that the best way to predict the future is to invent it through systematic goal-setting and goal-getting. The "goalmaking" process creates a self-fulfilling process all its own – one that is characterized by personal achievement, satisfaction and success.

> **"Goalmaking" is ground breaking.**

Once you get the goal-setting process down, it becomes a habit. You will discover that the fears and pain of resistance will fade away. You will become stronger in mind and enabled to stay focused on your achievable goal. Before we get into the steps of setting goals, let's affirm the following:

Goals:

- give you a sense of direction
- create discipline in your life
- ensure motivation in your life
- generate enthusiasm
- help build your confidence
- enhance your performance
- make you accountable
- create opportunities

The timeline for goal-setting will vary. It ranges from short-range goals, medium-range goals, and long-range goals:

1. Short -range goals range from 30 to 180 days.

   (One of the purposes of setting short-range goals is to experience immediate results that will be identified as stepping stones in reaching long-range goals.)

2. Medium-range goals vary from 6 months to one year.

3. Long-range goals vary from one year to five years and beyond.

If you want to control your future, you must create a plan that involves all three goal ranges. If you don't set personal, scholastic or career goals, someone will set them for you. The thought of being someone's puppet has absolutely no appeal to me. I believe it has no appeal to you, either, or else you wouldn't have selected this book. So, I hope you will take "goalmaking" seriously, because it is part of backpacking for success.

> *If you don't set a goal for yourself,*
> *someone else will.*

Goals should never be perceived as a burden, but as a direction on which to focus your knowledge, skills and energy. Have fun during this process. Consider getting your family or peers involved in planning your goals.

My son, Marcus, came up to me one day and wanted me to buy him a bicycle. I used it as a perfect opportunity to teach him about "goalmaking."

"Okay, Marcus, this is what we'll do. We'll look through different brands and see which one you like the best. Then we will set a bike-purchase goal."

At the time I was a salesperson in residential real estate sales, so I told him, "For every sale I make, I will put $10 toward the purchase of your bicycle."

Everyday when I got home from work, Marcus would ask how many sales I had made that day. He bugged me every day about my sales until our goal was accomplished. He was my accountability partner.

> **A Backpack Keeper:** It's never too early or too late to set realistic stretch goals.

# Goal-Setting Leads to Goal-Getting

The wonderful thing about accomplishing goals is how the whole goal attainment business transforms the "goalmaker." Merely achieving goals by themselves, like accomplishment for accomplishment's sake, will never make us truly happy. The magic is in who we become as we overcome our fears, disappointments and doubts on the path toward each goal's attainment. "Goalmaking" is a character-building process.

It gives you a deep sense of fulfillment, accomplishment and satisfaction.

One of the most helpful insights I have received about the whole nature of goal attainment is this: goals aren't accessories in life. They're necessities. That's why I've selected goals as one of the key tools to place in your backpack. It doesn't matter if you're 18 or 80 – you'll always need "something" to get up for each day, "something" to work toward, "something" to pursue that brings satisfaction and meaning to your life.

> *It doesn't take much time –*
> *20 minutes per day*
> *times*
> *5 days per week*
> *equals*
> *100 minutes per week*
> *times*
> *52 weeks per year*
> *equals*
> *5,200 minutes per year*
> *divided by*
> *60 minutes per hour*
> *equals*
> *86.5 hours per year*
> *to reach the next level.*

The venerable humorist George Burns understood the significance of setting realistic, life-affirming goals. Even in his late 90's, he set five and ten-year goals. When asked to sum up his philosophy on the importance of goals, he once replied, "You have to have something to get you out of bed. At my age, I can't do anything in bed, anyway. The most important thing is to have a direction (in which) you're headed."

**A Backpack Keeper:** "Goalmaking" is not an accessory; it is a necessity if you expect to succeed.

# Goals Are Dreams With a Timeline

All of us are what I call "multi-storied" people. By that I mean, all of us have many areas requiring personal and professional growth. I have found the following exercises to be *extremely* beneficial when it comes to improving many areas of my life. I believe you will too, if you'll take a few minutes to complete three of the most valuable self-assessments you will ever make. I'm not kidding! Record your responses in this book, or photocopy these pages and enlarge them somewhat, so you and those you love can benefit from them. Make it a family exercise. When you're ready, begin.

# The Old Me
## (Five Years Ago)

Next to each of the following "compartments" of your lifestyle five years ago, describe what you accomplished in that "compartment" and/or what that area looked like at that time in your life. Then rate yourself, on a scale from 0 to 10, on how well you did in that "compartment." (Zero represents a low level of goal attainment, 10 means you accomplished a considerable amount of goals in that area.)

| Compartment | Accomplishments/Description | Rating |
|---|---|---|
| Physical Health: | _____ | ___ |
| Mental Health: | _____ | ___ |
| Emotional Health: | _____ | ___ |
| Educational Achievements: | _____ | ___ |
| Career Accomplishments: | _____ | ___ |
| Financial Health: | _____ | ___ |
| Spiritual Development: | _____ | ___ |
| Travel: | _____ | ___ |

## The Present Me
## (Today)

For comparison's sake, see how far you've come, or failed to come, in each of these key "compartments." Describe your accomplishments and rate yourself again, on the same 0 to 10 scale, describing your accomplishments and/or what you're like in each of these "compartments" TODAY.

| Compartment | Accomplishments/Description | Rating |
| --- | --- | --- |
| Physical Health: | _____ | |
| | _____ | ____ |
| Mental Health: | _____ | |
| | _____ | ____ |
| Emotional Health: | _____ | |
| | _____ | ____ |
| Educational Achievements: | _____ | |
| | _____ | ____ |
| Career Accomplishments: | _____ | |
| | _____ | ____ |
| Financial Health: | _____ | |
| | _____ | ____ |
| Spiritual Development: | _____ | |
| | _____ | ____ |
| Travel: | _____ | |
| | _____ | ____ |

## The Future Me
## (Five Years From Now)

How will your profile look five years from now? Describe your accomplishments in each of the key "compartments" and then rate the anticipated level of energy, commitment and accomplishment you expect to achieve in each of these areas, on the same 0 to 10 point scale.

| __Compartment__ | __Accomplishments/Description__ | __Rating__ |
|---|---|---|
| Physical Health: | _____ | |
| | _____ | \_\_\_\_\_ |
| Mental Health: | _____ | |
| | _____ | \_\_\_\_\_ |
| Emotional Health: | _____ | |
| | _____ | \_\_\_\_\_ |
| Educational Achievements: | _____ | |
| | _____ | \_\_\_\_\_ |
| Career Accomplishments: | _____ | |
| | _____ | \_\_\_\_\_ |
| Financial Health: | _____ | |
| | _____ | \_\_\_\_\_ |
| Spiritual Development: | _____ | |
| | _____ | \_\_\_\_\_ |
| Travel: | _____ | |
| | _____ | |

What you have just set in motion, by completing "The Future Me" assessment, is a preliminary list of goals in eight critical areas of your life. I highly recommend your getting even more serious about setting goals, and add more "compartments" to this list. Brainstorm as many additional goals as you can over the next couple of days. Create a goal journal. Determine which goals are long-term and which are short-term. Select 16 goals, one or two from each "compartment," and list them on the first page of your journal. These special goals are your "Sweet Sixteen" goals. They will be the ones you will spend your time and energy on. As you accomplish one, replace it with another goal from your lengthy list of goals, so you will always have 16 special goals to focus on.

Remember, goals are dreams with a timeline. If you will commit to this process for one year, you will be absolutely amazed at how much the "Present You" will accomplish for the "Future You." It will be a year well spent. As Victor Hugo said, "There is nothing like a dream to create the future. Utopia today, flesh and blood tomorrow." That's why setting goals is so important. Goal-setting turns possibilities into probabilities, and consistent goal-getting transforms probabilities into realities.

---

**A Backpack Keeper:** People who go through life without goals are practicing the art of living life by stumbling around.

---

# From "Goalmaker" to Goal-Crafter

"Goalmakers" are a unique breed of people. They not only set goals and achieve them, they make a commitment to always be the best. People admire people who are good at what they do. My parents pounded it into my little head to do the best job at whatever I attempted. They told me that any boy could be a good student, good athlete, good friend, or good employee. They challenged me to go beyond just doing good work. They wanted me to do my best.

> ***Whatever you decide, decide to be the best.***

My dad's chosen profession was a janitor for the local county hospital. Today some folks refer to the profession as building maintenance, maintenance engineer or custodian. Dad preferred to be called a janitor. One day he started his own janitorial service. He built such a reputation that all the major businesses in our small town contracted his services. Soon he gained the reputation as the best janitor in the county. Today, they call it "best in class."

I will never forget hearing customers say, "George does such an outstanding job that after he finishes cleaning, you can eat off the floor." That would have to be a pretty clean floor, wouldn't you agree? All four of his sons grew up in the janitorial business. When each of us reached a certain age, Dad would take us to work and teach us the business. I was the youngest, so I had to wait my turn to join the team and gain his trust.

There were several levels of job descriptions, and each of us had to be proficient at each one. Once we mastered one job, we would be given the privilege to advance to the next job. I was 10-years old when Dad decided to allow me to help for the first time. Boy, was I excited! I knew I had gained his trust. My first job was to help pick up the trash off the floor and empty the trash cans in the building. Once I mastered this assignment, I graduated to the next job. I wanted to skip the next job and go to job number three, which was cleaning windows. (Would you like to guess what job number two was? If you guessed cleaning bathrooms, you were correct!) I tried to negotiate my way out of cleaning toilets, but my father wasn't buying it, and neither were my brothers. We didn't use rubber gloves back then. We had to take a rag in our hand and clean the toilet bowl. Yuk! I still get sick thinking about it.

Dad took me into the bathroom to give me my instructions. I began my negotiation. "Dad, do I really have to clean this bathroom? It's a mess."

"Not only do you have to clean this bathroom," Dad explained, "but when you're done, call me and I will inspect the entire bathroom and the job you did. And if by chance the toilet is not clean or does not meet our sanitary specifications, you will lick it clean."

When he walked out, I closed the door and locked it. I was terrified. I thought he was really going to make me lick it if it wasn't clean. I grudgingly proceeded to clean the bathroom floor, walls, bowl, sink and any other surface area I could think of. Every few minutes, Dad would knock on the door to see if I was ready for him to check my work.

I must have yelled, "Not yet!" dozens of times. Finally, 45 minutes later, I let him in to do his inspection.

After looking at each item, all he would say was, "Hmmmmm." When he got to the toilet bowl, I remember swallowing hard and thinking, *Please be clean. Please be clean!*

"Hmmmmm," he said. Then he looked me in the eye and said, "Good job, *mi hijo* (my son). That's a really good job." Then he walked out.

I smiled my relief and thought, *No bathroom licking for me today!*

Little did I know or realize during this time that he was purposefully teaching me lessons. I discovered that whatever job or assignment you accepted, you were to do the best you could. My dad wanted us to do the BEST and be the BEST. After that day, I became the best sweeper, mopper, duster and window cleaner in Dad's business. When I was 16-years old, I was allowed to contract my own side jobs.

> *The best people don't win nearly as often as the people who get along "best."*
> *(Harvey Alston)*

Turn back to "The Future Me" exercise on page 142. Pick one of the key compartments of your life and re-read what you recorded in the "Expected Accomplishments and Improvements" column. It should be an area where you expect to achieve close to a "10" in terms of your future accomplishments. Once you've made your selection, turn to the *"Goalmaker" Form* on page 147. Make a photocopy of the *"Goalmaker" Form* in this book, or download the 8x10 "Goalmaker" Form from my website: www.Jimmy Speaks.com.

Once you've manufactured a blank copy of the *"Goalmaker" Form,* write today's date in the space provided. Record the selection you chose from "The Future Me" exercise as your Goal Statement on the *"Goalmaker" Form.* You

**GOALMAKERS**

**My Goal**

Today's Date: _____

GOAL Statement

I will (commit): _____
                        Action Verb – Something I Can Measure

Within or by the following time period: _____

RESOURCES:

1. _____
2. _____
3. _____
4. _____

| STEPS TO REACH THIS GOAL | TIME REQUIRED COMPLETE | DATE TO BE COMLETED |
|---|---|---|
| 1. | | |
| 2. | | |
| 3. | | |
| 4. | | |
| 5. | | |

| POSSIBLE OBSTACLES | POSSIBLE SOLUTIONS |
|---|---|
| 1. | |
| 2. | |
| 3. | |
| 4. | |

By signing here, I commit to my goal and will do my best to stay focused....

✓ _____

147

will notice the Goal Statement starts off with the words "I will (Commit)." This is a positive statement that calls for intent and action on your part. Also note the word "will" and not "want."

On the line to the right of "Within or by the following time period," record a time period that is realistic and one that has a high expectation of success.

Next, under the "Resources" column, list the available resources that can increase your chances of success. By definition, a resource is: 1) something that can be drawn upon for aid or to take care of a need; 2) a means to accomplish something; 3) a source of strength; 4) something that is made available to you; 5) something that can be used as an advantage; 6) someone to whom one turns in time of need. Resources can be people, places or things that provide the support you need in your goal attainment process.

In the next section, "Steps to Reach This Goal," be as specific as you can. Brainstorm a list of steps on a separate sheet of paper, and then sequence them in the order in which you will need to accomplish them. Then transfer that prioritized list to the *"Goalmaker" Form.* Based on how much time you need, determine a completion date for each step.

You will no doubt face obstacles and pitfalls along the way. List any obstacles which might interfere with your progress. Obstacles can take many forms. They can be attitudinal, technological, social, material, geographical, ethical, etc. List anything you think would negatively affect your goal accomplishment. Generate possible solutions to combat each obstacle.

Robert Schuller puts it this way: "What is the cross but a minus (–) turned into a plus (+)." Booker T. Washington said, "You measure the size of the accomplishment by the obstacles you have to overcome to reach your goals." I agree again. So, spend some quality time on this. The more contingencies you uncover during the goal-writing phase, the greater your chances are of identifying alternatives and solutions that help guarantee your success. Repeat the commitment statement out loud at the bottom of the form, and sign it. You now have a signed personal "Goalmaker" contract.

Repeat this same process for each of the eight lifestyle compartments on "The Future Me" assessment. Complete two-to-three *"Goalmaker" Forms.* When you've achieved those goals, start another "Goalmaker" gold rush.

---

### *Goal power is Go power!*

---

You've got the "goalmaking" process now, so go for it. There's no excitement in mediocrity. There's no real enjoyment in the status quo. And there's certainly no fun in learning you've missed a once-in-a-lifetime opportunity. You've written your goals, now underwrite your goals by taking action. Remember: *If it is to be, it is up to me.* Expect to succeed. Make course adjustments if you have to, but stay focused on your goal. I can't emphasize enough that when you take your goals seriously – they'll take you seriously.

---

**A Backpack Keeper:** What you achieve in reaching your goals pales in comparison to what you become by reaching them.

---

# Backpack Wisdom

1. People who fail to plan, plan to fail.

2. The best way to predict your future is to invent it.

3. It's never too early or too late to set realistic stretch goals.

4. Goals are dreams with a timeline.

5. "Goalmaking" is not an accessory; it is a necessity.

6. Goals turn possibilities into probabilities.

# Commit to Excellence in Everything You Do

# Chapter 7

# Commit to Excellence in Everything You Do

*I'm a natural fighter. When I commit to something, I do it. If I'm in the middle of the ocean and I have to swim, I'm going to swim until I have to stop swimming.* (Julio Iglesias)

Regardless of the kind of success you are seeking, one of the hallmarks of your success will be the amount of commitment you are willing to put into it. Good intentions never made anyone successful. Putting those good intentions into action is a necessary ingredient in your success formula. Your actions must support your intentions. The intriguing thing about commitment is that the longer you persist, the more immersed you become, and the more immersed you become, the more emotionally invested you will become in the outcome. Persistence enables you to uncover talents and abilities you didn't even know you had so you can "swim until you have to stop swimming."

*Webster* defines commitment as: an obligation; a pledge; duty; a resolution to do something; a devotion. It certainly is those things and more. It is one of the litmus tests for your success in life. Because it is fueled by your attitude and belief in yourself, it is the one ingredient that overcomes obstacles and resistance. It can be your "stepping" stone or "stopping" stone!

In his book, *See You At the Top*, Zig Ziglar believes that we are "designed for accomplishment, engineered for success and endowed with the seeds of greatness." I agree wholeheartedly! That means that we are the only ones who can use our talents and abilities to accomplish our unique version of success. What we choose to do and what we elect not to do are matters of choice. Either we want to succeed or we don't. This is a sobering thought – and it is the fundamental message of this chapter.

Whether your dreams materialize instantly or take years to unfold, the only limit to what you can achieve in your life is the size of your commitment, the power of your commitment and the intensity of your commitment.

> **A Backpack Keeper:** Commitment
> is not a matter of chance,
> it is a matter of choice.

# You Cannot Blow an Uncertain Trumpet

People are more persuaded by the depth of your commitment and the attitude you project than any amount of logic, knowledge, power or position you possess. Father Theodore Hesburgh, the former President of Notre Dame

University, described the importance of unfailing commitment: "It's got to be a vision you articulate clearly and forcefully every day. You cannot blow an uncertain trumpet." You must become what management guru, Tom Peters, calls "a monomaniac with a mission." Monomaniacs are so focused and committed to their stated objectives that they refuse to be derailed, side-tracked, disappointed or dissuaded.

I'd like to introduce you to the Cortes Theory of Managing Commitments. When the explorer, Hermando Cortes, landed in Mexico in 1519, his troops wanted to return to Spain because their hearts were not in the immense military task at hand. They had met the enemy and were tired, frustrated and disillusioned at their lack of progress. They wanted to go home. Cortes ordered *all* of his ships burned and announced that he was marching forward. The psychological payoff produced a victory for Cortes and his army.

I use this historical fact to illustrate this point: commitment is more than wishful thinking, it is a contract with your future. In order to achieve what you want in life, you will have to burn the ships of doubt, fear, ridicule negativity, setbacks, procrastination and so on. Action conquers fear, destroys excuses and compromises setbacks. For *backpack* people, commitment means total involvement, absolute immersion and the willingness to "burn ships," if necessary!

> *Learning to listen to our feelings is the key to maintaining our commitment over the long haul.*

The care and feeding of your dream takes persistence, perseverance, passion and patience – but not necessarily in that order. You've got to stay turned-on and tuned-in to your dreams to keep the momentum going. Both your thoughts and feelings must be consistent and directed toward sustaining your commitment.

In his excellent book, *Emotional Intelligence*, Daniel Goleman introduces the concept of emotional intelligence which helps people understand the interconnectedness between thoughts, feelings and actions. It is written in such a way that parents, teachers and teens can gain life-changing insights. He believes it is possible to re-educate ourselves about the way we experience our feelings. I have found that to be true in my own life. I am constantly aware of my feelings and attitudes and know that although they may register in the brain, they are felt in the body. As a matter of fact, over 80% of our feelings are expressed nonverbally. (I've already mentioned the impact of "body language" in Chapter 5)

If you are making notes in the margin or highlighting certain sentences or paragraphs in this book, you may want to make this next statement one of your keepers. Learning to experience our feelings – to listen carefully to what they are telling us, and then to act purposefully and appropriately – is the key to maintaining our commitment over the long haul. Emotional mastery is a critical life-long skill. It is a prerequisite for maintaining the right attitudes and a necessity for staying on track with your goals and dreams.

**A Backpack Keeper:** Most people fail to see their dream come true because of a commitment eclipse.

155

# Will Power vs. Won't Power

The passion must show. You've got to show you care for your dream. You can't fake commitment. Abraham Lincoln said, "You can fool some of the people some of the time, but you can't fool all of the people all of the time." People can tell how committed you are by your actions. The people in the following stories were obsessed with their dreams and they showed it.

Debbie Fields, the founder of Mrs. Fields Cookies, sees herself as a cookie person. She always carried her product with her. Ray Kroc, the founder of McDonald's, saw the beauty in every hamburger bun. All his stories are about hamburger buns. Mr. Marriott, Sr., read every complaint card his corporation received for over sixty years. He loved the hotel business. Mary Kay Ash of Mary Kay Cosmetics loved her business and kept all of her top representatives in the pink. Frank Perdue loved chickens. Jan Carlzon idolizes on-time flights, demands stain-free trays and loves to see every plane leave the ground with passengers in every seat.

Obsessed with the various uses of his discovery, Charles Goodyear wore rubber clothing and shoes on the streets of New York and spent several fortunes creating rubber paraphernalia. Bette Nesmeth Graham, the founder of Liquid Paper white-out, left her secretarial job and took the risk as a single mother to experiment with a correcting fluid. She wanted to develop a suitable substitute for the smudges caused by carbon typewriter ribbons. Lee Trevino loves golf so much that he carries golf equipment with him wherever he goes, gives people golf pointers during regular conversations, and shows kids how to grip a golf club properly every chance he gets.

The feeling of *doing the right work*, coupled with a strong sense of having the right talents and committing to your life purpose, is an essential ingredient in keeping your dream alive.

In their classic book, *Living the Good Life*, Scott and Helen Nearing wisely propose that the ultimate purpose of working is not necessarily "to make a fortune, but to find our connection with the right work and commit ourselves to it." I believe they're on to something. Some people play by the numbers and for the numbers, but for other people, *backpack* people, the numbers are merely play.

> **People can tell how committed you are by your actions.**

*Backpack* people instinctively know what they must do with their time and energy. They exercise more *will* power than *won't* power. I am convinced that once you know what you want, you're more likely to discover how to get it because your will power is at such a high pitch.

People who seem to be totally committed to their dreams have a number of important things in common:

1. They have a strong sense of how their lives and work fit their dream.
2. They have an internal compass, their faith in God, which keeps them moving toward their dream.
3. They are aware of their talents and abilities as well as their weaknesses and limitations.
4. They are resilient and flexible in the midst of chaotic environments.
5. They have an incredible amount of energy and stamina, and their enthusiasm is infectious.
6. They seem to have a sense of imperviousness when it comes to burdens and hardships.
7. They have drive, determination and passion when it comes to taking care of their business because they have a lifestyle rich in purpose.

> **A Backpack Keeper:** Commitment is like duct tape – it holds the good days and the bad days together.

## The Drive to Thrive

Persistence is a "won't be denied" attitude, especially during those times when it seems everything is working against you. Great athletes like Tiger Woods, Lee Trevino, Michael Jordan, Nancy Lopez, Anika Sorenstein and Wayne Gretzky instinctively know when to elevate their games. Undaunted by what seems to be a hopeless situation, these athletes step up their game and achieve the impossible. In the words of Lee Trevino, one of golf's all-time great champions, "I don't think it was my swing that made me the player I was or am, I think it's just the heart and guts and the determination to succeed."

Simple actions can make a big difference. Jim Carey, famous comedian and actor, wrote a check to himself for quite a large amount of money. He believed in the power of suggestion and turned his positive attitude into a tangible action which reminded him every day to work toward the income he desired. Sometimes actions like Jim Carey's seem ridiculous or fanciful, but they are positive statements of an intense commitment to succeed. He turned wishful thinking into practical actions and accomplished the impossible. People like Jim Carey remind us that we, too, can achieve something we think is impossible by adopting the drive to thrive.

When ice skater Sarah Hughes was interviewed after her amazing Olympic gold medal performance in Salt Lake City, she told Scott Hamilton she had been inspired by the great figure skaters over the past ten years, including the phenomenally-talented Michelle Kwan, who she outskated for the Olympic gold medal. "Ever since I was six years old, I wanted to skate like Kristi (Yamaguchi), Tara (Lipinski) and Michelle (Kwan). I saw myself winning a gold medal at the Olympics," Sarah confirmed.

The sources of inspiration for Sarah were national record holders, world champion figure skaters and coaches who epitomized her ideals in women's figure skating.

She was inspired by parents and friends who believed in her. Sarah's drive to thrive inspires others to be the best they can be. It's a great example of how inspiration works.

Hundreds of young girls, barely able to stand on skates, flock to gymnasiums across America so they can be like Sarah Hughes, who at age sixteen is one of the youngest figure skating champions in Olympic history and the only woman skater to land two triple-triple jump combinations in competition as of this writing.

Both Sarah and Jim Carey have "I can" attitudes. They know the importance of thinking big. David Schwartz, in his book, *The Magic of Thinking Big*, describes it this way:

*Every step forward pays dividends. Success is determined not so much by the size of one's brain as it is the size of one's thinking...Thinking big does work magic. You can move a mountain with enough commitment and drive. The "I can" attitude generates the magic.*

A story about Lee Iacocca illustrates the essence of this skill. He wanted to add a convertible to Chrysler's automobile line. So he met with his engineers and instructed them to craft a model. They promised him they would have a prototype ready in nine months to a year. It is reported that Iacocca was not at all satisfied with giving birth to a new car design in their time frame. In typical Iacocca fashion, he ordered a prototype design by the end of the day, and the prototype itself by the end of the month.

By mid afternoon the project leader approached Lee with the sad news that his time requirement for producing a prototype was absolutely impossible. They would need at least six months. Iacocca was furious and immediately led the project leader to the plant floor, pointed to a Chrysler-in-progress and ordered the engineer to saw off the top of the car and have it delivered to the front of the building.

Iacocca then proceeded to conduct some market research of his own. He drove around Detroit in the sawed-off "prototype" and evaluated the response he got from passers-by. He ordered the car built by the end of the month.

As doubtful as this story sounds, it has been verified to be true. His actions sent shock waves throughout the engineering department. Wouldn't you agree? His message was loud and clear: If you work for me, you must have the drive to thrive. Iacocca knew that a manager's day-to-day behavior sends messages that either motivate people or stifle their enthusiasm. He had the "I can" attitude and wanted to instill the same attitude throughout the whole company. He was a *backpack* person. He knew the importance of commitment and he exemplified a "won't be denied" attitude in everything he did.

> **A Backpack Keeper:** If commitment is unaccompanied by talent, beating your head against a wall is more likely to give you a concussion than achieve your goal.

# Fall Forward

I am sure you have experienced failure and even rejection. I am sure you have, at one time or another, had a bad day, week or year. We all have. A few years ago I was having one of those challenging days. It was a month after my accident. I had fallen from the roof of our home and seriously injured my wrist and left shoulder. I am very thankful that I did not lose the use of my left arm and hand. I underwent three surgeries and some tough physical therapy.

One of my speaker friends, Ray Pelletier, heard about my accident and called to see how my recovery was going. I knew he called to cheer me up, but I was not in the mood. He could tell by the tone of my voice that I was not having a good day. I had a bad case of feeling sorry for myself, – you know – PLOM Disease.

He says, "Hey little brother, sounds like you're having it pretty rough. You need to practice what you teach and snap out of feeling sorry for yourself. You sound like your world has come to an end. It's like you're trying to achieve something and you've fallen flat on your face. Am I right, little brother?"

"Well, yes, Ray. In fact, I literally fell flat on my face."

"Jimmy, I believe that whenever you attempt something and fall flat on your face, it's good news."

"Wait a minute," I said. "How can you call falling flat on my face good news?"

Ray responded, "Well, you see Jimmy, when you fall flat on your face, you're falling forward."

I started laughing and I knew he was right. I reminded myself that we should always try to find the positive in the negative things we go through in life. Failure to me is only a brand of success I didn't like.

161

---

> **Failure to me is only a brand of success I didn't like.**

---

As I look back on my conversation with Ray, I remember his sound advice. But I also remember something I did to take the edge off what I was going through. I laughed! I immediately felt the tension leave. So my advice to you is have the courage to laugh at yourself when you're taking yourself too seriously.

In a poll taken by *Entertainment Weekly* magazine, 85% of the movie-going audience wants to laugh and be entertained; 5% prefer a movie that makes them cry; and 4% want a movie that frightens them enough to scream. It is obvious from this study – and other qualified research – that most people prefer to laugh instead of cry. They prefer happiness over sadness and joy over fear.

So give yourself a lift right now. Give your immune system a boost. Before you read any further, laugh out loud. I'm serious. Laugh. LAUGH OUT LOUD. LAUGH HEARTILY. Rear your head back and belt one out. You may feel silly at first. But laugh a belly laugh. Every time you laugh heartily, you elevate your immune system. And elevating your immune system helps you meet the challenges associated with your commitment. Laughter is connected to your neurology and your energy, which is connected to the amount of energy you have to spend on your commitments. So fortify your health and energize your commitment by lifting each corner of your mouth frequently and robustly.

Very quickly now, rate how often you laugh heartily each day on a scale from 0 to 10, where 0 means no laughing and 10 is the heartiest of laughs several times a day. How good are you at elevating your immune system? Whatever you rated your "laugh meter" – double it today. Everyone needs at least a couple of good belly laughs each day. If you rarely laugh and gave yourself a "0," my heartfelt advice to you is to laugh several times a day whether you want to or not – because you need to laugh.

> *Laughter is connected to your neurology, which is connected to the amount of energy you have to spend on your commitments.*

In the hilarious movie, *City Slickers*, Billy Crystal plays a character called, Mitch Robins, a disillusioned radio advertising salesman who decides to vacation at a Western dude ranch to "find himself." He has his wife's support and before he goes, she tells him, "You need to find your smile." She insists that he needs to lighten up, to rediscover his sense of humor.

She's right, of course, and over the course of the ninety-minute film, Mitch learns the value of laughter and that he should not take himself too seriously. At the end of the movie, nothing visibly in his life has changed. He still has the same boring job, the same family and the same big city problems, but on the inside everything has changed. He has a different outlook on life. He has found his smile – a sense of joy and wonder have returned.

**A Backpack Keeper:** Good belly laughs help us stomach our commitments.

Many people today are in the same "place" Mitch was in the beginning of the film – smileless and commitment deficient. Boredom and monotony rule their lives. They feel hollow and joyless. They find themselves "going through the motions" day in and day out.

Take the following quiz. I call it your *Smile Quotient*:

1. Where did you leave your beautiful smile?
   ❏ at home  ❏ at work
   ❏ under the weight of your last disappointment

2. How often do you smile?
   ❏ rarely  ❏ sometimes  ❏ frequently

3. Are you having more or less fun than you did a year ago?
   ❏ more  ❏ less  ❏ about the same

4. How often does your smile become infectious laughter?
   ❏ rarely  ❏ sometimes  ❏ often

No matter how you scored on your "Smile Quotient," think of at least two people who have put a smile on your face this past week. Ray Pelletier put a smile on my face when I needed it. Write, call or email them and tell them how much you appreciate them. Thank them for their ability to make you smile. Do it now before you read another word.

As we wrap up this chapter, I would like to encourage you to spend some time with my *Hola 100 Backpack Challenge*. It is a game you can play with yourself over the next 21 days. I promise that if you make a commitment to play by the rules, you will transform your attitude and see a huge payback in your health, your relationships and your life. So, let the game begin!

## Hola 100 Backpack Challenge (Rules of the Game)

*Rule #1:* In the next twenty-one (21) consecutive days, repeat to yourself "If it is to be, it is up to me." at least twenty-one times each day. You can repeat this powerful phrase aloud or mentally.

*Rule #2:* When you catch yourself thinking negatively about yourself for any reason, smile, take a deep breath and inhale slowly. Then repeat "If it is to be, it is up to me." As your first line of attack, ask yourself these questions: a) What is it about this situation that causes me to doubt or criticize myself? b) How can I engineer a more positive outcome next time?

Record your responses and then evaluate your answers under each question. Turn negatives into positives by replacing "If it is to be" in the ten word power expression with a positive "I am" expression. For example: Turn "I totally lack the confidence to do this well," into "If I am to be totally confident, it is up to me." Turn "I'm so stupid," into "If I am to look at this more intelligently, it is up to me."

*Rule #3:* For the next twenty-one consecutive days, make certain your whole focus is on positive outcomes instead of negative consequences. Every time you turn a negative thought into a positive one, say Hola 100. (Remember the numerical equivalent to the word attitude is 100% – see Chapter 2.)

*Rule #4:* If you backslide – that is, if you find your-self slipping a little too much into self-demeaning criticism, you will need to do two things: a)Realize that discipline is not the same thing as punishment; and b)Talk yourself into keeping a positive outlook no matter what happens.

If you continue to dwell on the negative to the point of distraction, you must start your twenty-one day program all over again. The goal of the Hola 100 Backpack Challenge is to focus on positive outcomes by repeating, "If it is to be, it is up to me," as often as you can for twenty-one consecutive days. You must honor the start vs. restart process until you've elimi-nated any negative attitudes for the duration of this challenge. My hope is that you will be able to elimi-nate negative thoughts and attitudes altogether and keep your commitment to your dream.

*Rule #5:* At the end of each successful day of stay-ing positive and repeating "If it is to be, it is up to me" at least twenty-one times, celebrate your success by saying **Hola 100!**

# Backpack Wisdom

1. Commitment is not a matter of chance, it's a matter of choice.

2. Commitment is more than wishful thinking, it's a contract with your future.

3. Commitment means total involvement, absolute immersion, a willingness to go the extra mile.

4. Backpack people exercise more WILL POWER than WON'T POWER.

5. Persistence is a "won't be denied" attitude.

6. If you fall flat on your face, it means you're falling forward.

7. Good belly laughs help us stomach our commitments.

B

A

C

K

P

A

C

**K**eep Dreaming Big

# Chapter 8

# Keep Dreaming Big

*When you cease to dream, you cease to live.* (Malcolm S. Forbes)

Remember when you were a kid and how you would sit around with your friends and talk about your dreams? I want you to know that I still have that small kid inside of me. It doesn't matter whether you are 5, 25, 55 or 105, never stop dreaming. Hang on to your dreams. Don't let anyone, including yourself, discourage you from having dreams about what you want your life and career to be. I'd like to share a dream with you. Before I die, I'd like to have visited and spoken in 5,000 schools. As of today, I have spoken in over 700 schools. I've got a long way to go, don't you agree? But it's a wonderful way to go! I wouldn't want to be doing anything else.

Is my dream an impossibility? To me, it isn't. As long as I have breath and ability, I will speak at one school at a time. At every presentation I give, there are those who are inspired and challenged to reach their goals and dreams. I feel very fortunate to be in a position to influence so many students, teachers, principals and counselors. As I've said before, I take my responsibility seriously. When I first formulated the vision for my speaking business, the words of Helen Keller helped to solidify my focus in pulling out all the stops to make this business a success. She said: "I am only one; but still I am one. I cannot do everything, but still I can do something; I will not refuse to do the something I can do."

You've heard it said another way throughout this book: *If it is to be, it is up to me.* My dream is to speak in 5,000 schools before I get to the Pearly Gates. What's your dream?

All of us have dreams. We all want to believe deep down in our souls that we have a special purpose, that we are put here to make a difference, that we can help make the world a better place to live, that we can be the person we're meant to be. Yet for many of us, those dreams have become so vague and watered down by the frustrations and routines of daily life that we put them on the back burner and forget about them.

Far too many people have decided to die with the music in them. Many others have lost the will to dream at all. My guess is that you aren't one of them or you wouldn't have picked up this book. Your desire to learn how to be more successful has brought you to this book. It is the invisible hand that guides you. I know that no matter where you are in life, no matter what your status, power and position are, deep inside of you there lies a belief that you are destined for some type of greatness, some measure of happiness and some level of accomplishment.

In the movie, *Grumpy Old Men*, Jack Lemmon's 94-year-old father tells him that the only thing you ever regret in life are the risks you failed to take. And one of the most important risks you cannot fail to take is the risk of becoming what you are meant to be. You touch your future every time you take a step toward your dream, so you can look back on your life regret-free.

> **A Backpack Keeper:** You touch the future every time you take a step toward your dream.

Keep dreaming even if you are the only one who believes in your dream. Famous health education and enthusiast, Jack LaLanne, studied pre-med in college and planned to become a medical doctor. However, he realized that the medical profession was focused on recovery after illness instead of prevention before illness. He was interested in helping people prevent illness by maintaining a healthy lifestyle centered on personal fitness. That was his dream.

At age twenty-one, he opened the nation's first health studio in an old brick office building in Oakland, California. The sports equipment he invented is standard issue in health spas today. He was the first to encourage women, people with physical disabilities and the elderly to exercise for health.

His methods were criticized by the medical profession, the sports community and the media – until it was obvious that LaLanne was on to something. His dream sustained him for fifty years. When he was asked recently what made his fitness program so successful, he said, "I understand the working of the body, the muscles and bones, the nerves… What I was doing then, and continue to do now, is scientifically correct…starting with a healthy diet – and today everyone knows it. It was my dream of a healthy America that carried me through."

> ### *Keep dreaming even if you're the only one who believes in it.*

Jean Nidetch, a 214-pound New York housewife and mother, decided she needed to lose weight. She also knew she needed help to lose weight. So, she invited six over-weight friends to meet weekly in her small Queens apartment in June of 1961. They discussed their mutual weight problems and monitored each other's promises, diets and weight gains or losses.

Support groups of this type were almost nonexistent in the early 1960's, but word of her support group spread rapidly. By the end of the year, 50 people squeezed themselves into her tiny apartment for an opportunity to speak about their weight problems. "The only requirement we had for attendance," reported Jean, "was that everyone had to BHOC (Bring Her Own Chair)!"

In May of 1963, a little less than two years later, at a respectable 132 pounds, Jean incorporated her idea and announced the first public meeting of Weight Watchers. Today, Weight Watchers International is a thriving billion-dollar business with offices in nearly 40 countries.

Art Fry dreamed of turning his simple invention into a bigger success. He wanted to help himself to his dream, but he wanted his dream to help others. Do you know Art Fry? I'll bet you've used his Post-It® notes. That's right. He is the 3M Corporation engineer who invented Post-It® notes. Here's how he turned a dream into reality. While singing with his church choir, he kept losing his place in the hymnal, because his bookmark kept slipping out of sight. He used the bookmarks to help ease the chore of finding the next song to be sung. He tried folding the page edges, but that tactic didn't work well either. The other choir members expressed similar concerns. His frustration drove him to do what he does best – practice chemical engineering.

Art came up with a bookmark that had a patch of stickum on one side. His idea worked so well that all the other choir members wanted sticky bookmarks. Art decided to look for other applications, and created stickum notepads. The management at 3M didn't warm up to Art's idea at first. The secretarial pool did, however, and so did hundreds of 3M employees. Eventually, 3M built a multi-billion dollar business out of Art Fry's multi-colored Post-It® notes.

> *Help yourself to your dream, but let your dream help others.*

When people dream big and feel they can make a difference by using their talents to improve a situation for themselves and others, they will likely succeed where others have failed. Envisioning something which helps others seems to be the key. Oftentimes "dreamers" are people who turn negative experiences into positive opportunities.

A young girl who grew up in rural Mississippi dreamed of becoming a TV news personality. Although she had an extremely unhappy childhood, including abuse, she held on to her media dream. She became a rebellious and uncontrollable teenager. As a last resort, her mother sent her to live with her father. Vernon Winfrey and his wife, Zelma, were disciplinarians. They taught Oprah the importance of education, discipline and fairness.

Oprah finished high school and entered Tennessee State University. She majored in speech communications and landed a job at WTVF-TV in Nashville before she graduated. She became the first African-American news anchor at the station. In 1976, she joined the staff at WJZ-TV in Baltimore, MD, and co-anchored the *Six O'Clock News.*

Several years later, Oprah hosted the talk show *AM Chicago,* which was renamed *The Oprah Winfrey Show.* Eventually, she purchased her own talk show from Capital Cities/ABC and it quickly became the number-one talk show in America. She describes her success this way: "I had a vision I could succeed at anything I decided to do. You have to believe you can be whatever your heart desires and be willing to work for it."

> *Dreamers are people who turn negative experiences into positive opportunities.*

People who construct great visions, whether they are fitness gurus, chemical engineers, talk show hosts, students or housewives, are great dreamers. They make their dreams come true. Making your dreams come true involves making a series of choices based on a series of serious questions. I believe the following questions will help guide you toward answers that will make your dreams come true. Take some quality time right now to answer these questions:

1. Is my dream the right dream for me?

2. Will it help me be a better me and make the world a better place in which to live?

3. What skills, talents, experience, education and abilities do I possess or need to realize my dream?

4. How can I measure my success?

5. Am I energized by my dream, no matter how tired I am or busy I get?

6. Am I keeping the small promises I make to myself?

7. Will I feel incomplete and unfulfilled if I don't realize my dream?

> **A Backpack Keeper:** Put your common sense in gear before you put your dreams in motion.

# From Caterpillar to Butterfly

Have you ever stopped to think what separates those individuals who become great from those who remain average – those who exceed expectations from those who settle for mediocrity? Throughout my life and career, I have studied many individuals in the area of greatness. Please allow me to take you on a journey of metamorphosis and transformation.

It was a beautiful Houston afternoon – sunny, with a temperature in the mid-70's and low humidity. I was sitting outside on our patio, enjoying a rare summer breeze. All of a sudden, a butterfly landed across the patio table from where I was seated. It occurred to me that the butterfly journey from caterpillar to butterfly represented the difference between greatness and average. What came to my mind was the metamorphosis of the butterfly. I started to think about applying the same analogy to human beings, and refer to it

175

as the metamorphosis of a half-awake human being to a wide-awake dreamer. Let me explain.

As you know, butterflies don't start life as butterflies. The butterfly goes through stages of metamorphosis. The butterfly starts as a larva. Have you ever seen a larva? Larvae are not all that cute; in fact, they are kind of ugly. It's like you and I when we were born. We weren't all that cute either. Then the larva grows into a caterpillar. A caterpillar's chief occupation in this world is eating. As long as the caterpillar eats, it is happy and content.

Suppose we take a closer look at two caterpillars. Let's call them George and Sam. George and Sam go about their lives hanging out and eating, kind of like you and I shortly after we're born. All we want to do as babies is eat and sleep and crawl around. As you may be aware, the skin of the caterpillar is not elastic. It does not stretch and the caterpillar will eventually have to shed its skin. As it sheds its skin, it gets a new one.

One day I stepped out the front door of my home and noticed a caterpillar moving along the sidewalk. It was dragging something, so I leaned over to inspect it more closely. The caterpillar's caboose was its own skin! I also noticed something very significant. Once the caterpillar shed its skin, it *never looked back*. It just kept moving forward to its next destination.

Much like the caterpillar, we must must shed our "skins." I'm not talking about losing our epidermis or flaking off the dead skin from our sunburn. The "skins" I'm referring to are bitterness, unforgiveness, grudges, selfishness, guilt, anger, doubt, low self-esteem and other negative emotions that hold us back. Once we shed those skins, we must never look back. We've got to put our positive *backpack* skins on, like love, forgiveness, confidence, self-esteem, courage and grace. Then we, too, can move forward in our journey of success.

Let's get back to George and Sam. As they continue their journey in life, they become the best of buddies. They share their lives, limbs, leaves and meals. Then, all of a sudden, George starts to feel different inside. He senses there is a change coming in his life. He doesn't know what it is, but it doesn't matter because he trusts himself. As he continues his journey, he meanders into a butterfly crossing. He notices that there are hundreds of beautiful butterflies. These beautiful butterflies are full of the most vibrant colors he has ever seen.

He senses his own butterfly nature. In his excitement, he turns to his buddy Sam. Lifting one of his spindly legs upward, he shouts, "Hey, Sam! Look. Please look. Something tells me that you and I have one of those butterflies inside of us. I just know it! Trust me, we gotta go and become butterflies."

"Are you crazy? If God wanted us to be a butterfly, we would have been born that way. Forget it, George. Let's go and find something to eat," Sam said, annoyed at George's exuberance.

"No, no, no, Sam. We gotta pay our dues and let our dreams come true."

George leaves Sam behind and moves toward his dream. He makes his way up a little twig, letting his instincts guide him. He starts to weave a strand of silk and attaches himself to the twig. He hangs there suspended in the air. Then the silk starts to cover his entire body, and he begins to form a cocoon.

Right before the completion of the cocoon, before the small opening at the end is sealed, George has a thought. He says to himself, *Wait! Can I change my mind and not go through this process? I don't know how it ends. I want to be a butterfly. How is this cocoon going to help?* But then he trusts his instincts, and settles into his new situation.

In this phase of the metamorphosis, George feels very secure in his cocoon. He is there to become the creature he is meant to be. He is alone. Then a small opening appears at the end of the cocoon. George is ready to exit the cocoon. He has to use every bit of strength and energy he can muster to emerge from his cocoon.

As George emerges and sits idle on the twig, his wings are still matted against his body. He is very susceptible to the predators that dine on insects and butterflies. As George perches on the twig, his wings start to open. Finally they span to their full maturity. George can't believe how great he feels and how good he looks. But he doesn't know he can fly. The following thoughts cross his mind: *The cocoon is gone. I'm clinging tightly to this tiny twig. I'm staring in awe at the giant rainbow wings which unfold above me. I wonder if I have the courage to fly.*

The wind blows George off the twig. *Ah...ah...ah,* George thinks when his wings began to move. Wow! To his surprise, he can fly!

As George flies around, he looks down at the ground and sees someone he recognizes. *It's Sam, my old buddy!*

He lands next to Sam and guess what Sammy is up to? Eating, of course! George said, "Hey, Sam, wuz up, dude?"

"Who are you?" asks Sam.

"It's me, George. Don't you recognize me? Look into my eyes."

"George, it is you! Where did you buy that suit?"

"No, Sam. It's not a suit. It's me! You have one of these inside you, too!"

"Really, George? Are you sure?"

There is a moment of silence. Then Sam said, "Hey, George, can I go hang next to your cocoon?"

George's response was immediate. "Better yet, Sammy, why don't you get on my back and I'll give you a ride up to the cocoon."

George showed his friend the vacant cocoon and told Sam about his own butterfly nature. He explained that someday soon Sam would be able to fly, too.

"You mean I'll be able to fly like you?" Sam chorused.

George nodded and demonstrated his flying skills by showing several of his favorite maneuvers.

"Wow," said Sam. "That's marvelous! I can't wait to do that myself."

"You will," said George. "You will – in your own good time. Just hang on to your dream."

---

**Being the first in anything is not worthwhile if you don't open doors for others.**

---

As human beings, you and I can learn a lesson from George. We must realize that once we make a commitment to become our dreams, there is no turning back. We must metamorphosize from who we are into who we can become. It is based on the transformational power of the phrase: *If it is to be, it is up to me.*

Like George, we may be alone when we decide to set our dreams into action. Like George, we have to make a decision to step out on faith and move forward.

I read somewhere that a small boy discovered a butterfly emerging from its cocoon. After a short period of time, the youngster was concerned about the length of time it was taking the butterfly to exit its cocoon and fly away. Feeling sorry for the helpless butterfly, he decided to help free it from the cocoon. With one hand, he held the cocoon and in the other hand he pulled the butterfly out and laid it on the ground. He waited for the butterfly to fly away. Unfortunately, he didn't realize that struggle is part of the metamorphosis process. The moment the boy forcefully pulled the butterfly out of the cocoon, he terminated the natural metamorphosis process. Instead of helping the winged creature, the youngster damaged the fragile wings. The butterfly was unable to fly and became vulnerable to predators. You see, the wings of the butterfly are matted against its body because the fluids have not started to flow to complete the development of the wings.

You and I are also susceptible to certain kinds of predators – like discouragers who tell us that we have no future, no goals, no ability. Our own negative thoughts, lack of self-esteem, doubts and poor self-image are also predators. The butterflies that struggle the longest and hardest are the ones that live the longest. They are the ones that are the strongest. We, too, have our struggles in life. It takes commitment and hard work to reach our dreams.

Can you relate? I sure can. Having the faith to step forward into the unknown is not easy. But once we have paid our dues, we are ready to experience the rewards of all of our hard work.

One of the things I like about butterflies is their freedom to fly throughout the world and see its beauty. They get to enjoy the most beautiful flowers. When they land on a flower, they extract the best part of the flower – the nectar. Gathering the best from the flower is a privilege. We, too, can enjoy the best things in life once we become the person we are meant to be. When the butterfly migrates from flower to flower, the pollen is gathered on the tips of its legs, allowing it to distribute the pollen from one plant to another. This process is referred to as pollination. Both the butterfly and the plant benefit from this process since the pollination produces more flowers.

I'd like to make one more point before we leave this story. George showed Sam what he, too, could become. He reaffirmed Sam's butterfly nature. He encouraged his friend to hang on to his dream. He was a model and mentor for Sam. That is our role, too, as *backpack* people. Once we have achieved a certain level of excellence, we have an obligation to share that expertise with others. Our mentorship can help others realize their dreams.

**A Backpack Keeper:** It is not enough that you're striving toward a dream. The question is: Toward what kind of dream are you striving?

## Never Give Up

Eight years ago, I saw a cartoon that depicted a whooping crane with a frog in its beak. Half of the frog's body was in the crane's mouth. The only thing keeping the crane from swallowing the frog was the tenacity of the frog. He had placed his "hands" around the neck of the crane in a choke hold. He knew as long as he maintained this choke hold, the crane couldn't swallow him. The cartoon's caption read, "Never Give Up." I've shown that cartoon hundreds of times in my presentations. What a great illustration to encourage people to never give up.

One day, I was speaking to a group of 400 fourth graders. After the assembly, a young girl approached me and said, "Mr. Jimmy, why are you picking on that bird?" (The bird she was referring to was the crane in the cartoon.)

I was confused, so I asked her to explain. I am always learning from our youth.

She said, "Well, you see, Mr. Jimmy, that bird ain't going to give up, either!"

What an incredible insight from a fourth grader, wouldn't you agree? It is the crane's nature to eat frogs. But frogs want to survive, too. She saw both sides of the equation. What I learned from that sweet fourth grader that day was this: Refuse to be pulled in by the gravity of any situation in which you find yourself. No matter how hopeless a situation appears, you've got to hang on until you outlast the negative "pull" of any problem or hardship that seems to devour your future. You must not give in or give up.

If the crane represents an all-consuming negative thought, choke it out. If the crane symbolizes the debilitating effects of an illness or bad habit that seems to control your life, choke it out, squeeze it until it lets go. If the crane represents some kind of ominous fear that has eaten away at your confidence and self-esteem, reach out and take hold of it. Squeeze every ounce of life out of the fear. Refuse to give in to it. If prejudice, drugs, lies or hatred want to swallow you up and make you one of them, refuse to become a part of it, no matter how much ridicule or peer pressure you have to face. Like the frog in the cartoon example, squeeze the negative problem until it lets go.

Why do so many people never realize their dreams? Why do they get swallowed up by missed opportunities, fears, doubts and criticisms? Why do they give in to adversity and suffocate their dreams? Author and national bestseller Lucinda Bassett has this to say about people who have never realized their dreams:

*Some people deny their dreams, simply because the responsibility that comes with having what they want scares them. They secretly feel inadequate. They are afraid that if they were put to the test and really had to perform, they could not live up to anyone's expectations, especially their own...They see themselves as failures...They sabotage opportunities that could create success...They end up making choices not to go after certain dreams because of their lack of...self-confidence.*

One of the reasons why people don't reach the success they believe they should have in life is because they have no **G.U.T.S.** Heavy statement? Yes, it is. Let's see what the word GUTS stands for: **Giving Up Too Soon.** It is always too soon to quit. NEVER GIVE UP!

*No GUTS= Giving Up Too Soon*

Therefore, never give up on yourself and never give up on your:

| | |
|---|---|
| family | dreams |
| friends | commitment |
| goals | country |
| confidence | ability to forgive yourself |
| skills | ability to forgive others |
| attitude | spirituality |
| courage | employer |
| education | teachers |

You may want to add to this list. It is not meant to be all inclusive, so there may be special life issues that you don't want to give up on. List them in the margin or in your journal or diary. Let your guts carry your feet and let your feet carry you toward your dream.

In the movie, *Dead Poet's Society*, Robin Williams plays Professor John Keating, who has returned to the prep school he attended as a youngster. His mission is to teach his students about English literature *and* about the richness of curiosity and independent thinking. Throughout the film, he constantly urges them toward self-discovery.

At one dramatic juncture, he leaps on his desk and shouts, "*Carpe Diem*" (seize the day). He repeats the injunction "*Carpe Diem.* Why do I stand here?" Then he answers his own question: "I stand here to remind myself, and you, that we must constantly force ourselves to look at things differently…The world looks different from up here. Try it. All of you." With those words, he invites the students to stand on their desks.

Your world will look different, too, if you apply the principles in this book. The only thing that stands between you and your dreams is YOU. Robin Williams stood on his desk in the movie and urged his students to look at things differently – to seize the day! I'm *standing* on the *Eight Backpack Principles* outlined in this book and urging you to believe in ten powerful words:

## "IF IT IS TO BE, IT IS UP TO ME."

**A Backpack Keeper:** Your parents have left you a road map, your teachers have left you a road map, other important people in your life have left you a road map – but you still have to travel the road yourself.

184

# Backpack Wisdom

1. You touch the future every time you take a step toward your dream.

2. Dreamers are people who turn adversities into advantages.

3. Help other people realize their dreams while you are pursuing yours.

4. Never give up on yourself or your dream.

5. The only thing that stands between you and your dream is YOU.

# Backpack Feedback

ote: As you read these letters, know that they have inspired me. They also confirm the fact that I am at the right place at the right time in my speaking profession. I want you to know that I am only a vehicle delivering a message, and in no way want to be considered anything special or looking for any glory. Just knowing that I had a part in helping others is my reward. I have received thousands of letters from students, and I have read every one of them.

Please read each of the following. Perhaps there will be one which touches you, that encourages you to reach your next level of success in life. Perhaps you, too, will consider writing me a letter on some of the things you have learned that have made a difference in your life.

1. My name is Regina. I am 12 years old and in the seventh grade. I have an A.L.L. type of cancer. And I'm very glad that you came. I will never give up on getting well. But you helped me remember it more. So when I get sick or not feeling good after or not after chemo I will look at the piece of paper that you and I wrote Hope on. I will read it and never give up on getting better. I really enjoyed the assembly. Thank You.

   *Gina, Seventh Grade*

2. *All my friends are talking about your presentation. Thank you for coming to our school to help our whole school. I heard so much about your presentation and we want to hear more. Everyone said that you pulled their head out of their behind. But all of us want to thank you for your help and support. Maybe you can come next year.*

> *Artesia, Freshman in High School*

3. What I learned yesterday was very important. I learned that when someone makes fun of me I won't cry or try to commit suicide. I will just say, "Bad Seed, Bad Seed." Though people will always make fun of me, all I really have to do is ignore them. I learned that to succeed in life, I have to study hard and go through college. To do that I have to believe in myself and put the right stuff in my backpack. I may have problems at home, but I can be smart and stay in school. To graduate means everything to me. I hope I go toward the positive and not for the negative. So good luck to you in the future and I will always remember: If it is to be, It is up to me!

> Tuesday, Eighth Grade

4. Hi, my name is Novella. I am in the eighth grade and fourteen years old. I heard you speak. You helped me out a lot. By just that one talk. My grades are a lot better now. I'm not going with anyone. Because the guy I was going with wanted to do something I didn't want to do. And I got the nerve to say NO! Thank you for giving me the courage to stand up for myself. Also, you are very funny. I enjoyed listening to you.

> Novella, Eighth Grade

5. *To refresh you memory, this is the third time I have heard you speak. Where once again my admiration has reached its highest peak. If it hadn't been for you Jimmy, I don't know where I'd be, probably a dead statistic or just another hoodlum of our society. You've come to make me realize, and have opened my eyes to learn to set my standards high! As an Hispanic, I've come to feel that it is my responsibility to set the examples for other Latinos to see. If I hadn't heard you speak no doubt I would have been a high school drop out.*

*Your words have reached out to me. They've fueled me up and kept me going ever since from the start. I'm now a junior in college with a double major in sociology and psychology. Who knows where I'd be if you hadn't reached out to me.*

*Yes, you are a poet just in case you didn't know it! Your words are so strong that in a good sense they're very lethal. To the point where you make people think, and open their eyes to reality and take them away from fantasy land. People like you Jimmy, are the one's that have saved many lives, and for this I must thank our Lord.*

*Javier, Junior in College*

6. It was a pleasure to have you speak to our entire sixth-grade class again this year. You do very well in helping kids boost their self-esteem, examine their perceptions, think about others, and contemplate the future. I reviewed the essays they wrote after experiencing your presentation, and they are heart warming. Some of them bring tears to my eyes. One child this year wrote that he was contemplating suicide, but changed his mind because of you. We have him in counseling now. That one child makes all your efforts worthwhile.

Tom, Principal

188

7. I enjoyed what you had to say, you made me realize that even when it seems as though no one is there or can help that there will always be one person who cares. When you got serious and talked to us and asked about suicide I raised my hand, but afterwards I know it would never come true because of you and the promise we made about graduation. You have helped me in a way I never thought anyone could. I don't even know you well but if we ever meet again and I could help or save you I'd do it without anyone asking.

Eileen, Seventh Grade

8. Muchas Gracias por los consejos que usted vino a darnos este dia. Le dedico esta carta con mucho amor como avando usted vino. Yo antes de que usted viniera me sentía muy mal porque todos los niños me llamaban de nombres. Un dia yo fui a me case y le dije a me mama como usted le dijo a la esuela que yo Guiria morirme pero este dia ave usted. Viro yo comprendí muchas cosas y gracias a usted mes amigos me llaman por me nombre.

Como usted dijo: If it is to be, It is up to me

Eva, Sixth Grade

9. *Your presentation was great. Now I am not ashamed to ask for help, or carry my books to school. My grades have changed and my attitude has changed too. Now I know how to set goals thanks to your seminar. Setting goals has changed my whole outlook in life. Now I know what I want to be when I grow up. Your speeches were great. I think every student should know how to set goals. Can you come back and teach them?*

*Craig, Eighth Grade*

189

10. I really enjoyed your presentation. You were really funny and you got your message through to me. You taught me to believe in myself and to help others. Before I heard your presentation I was always shy and worried about what others thought about me. Then after I heard your presentation I learned to try my best and not to let anything interfere with my goals. You are the nicest man I have ever met. I also want to thank you for the way you changed my way of thinking positive. I really think it's good that you are going all over and talking to students because the message you are sending out is one every student should hear.

Jerry, Freshman in High School

11. Jimmy, I thought your seminar was great. It touched me and my classmates too. I have been having some problems at home. My mom has depression and my dad is disabled. My dad and me don't get along very well at all. After going to your seminar, I've been doing a lot better. I've been getting along with my dad pretty much. When I get mad at my dad, I just go listen to my tape you gave me. Then I come out of my room feeling like a new man. My dad tells me to do something and I just do it and my dad sits there astonished at my actions. I now have my mom listening to your tape and she seems to be in a better mood all the time. Because of your seminar, my life has changed drastically. Because of your tape my mom's life has changed drastically. Thanks for helping me and my family.

Josh, Seventh Grade

12. *Como esta usted, espero que bien. Ya que estoy muy, gracias a Dios. Aquí redigo lo siguiente. Le mando esta carta para decirle que me gusto como hablo y degustaron todo los consejos que dio, usted. Acerca do no salirse de la escuela o acerca do las drogas. Porque yo antes pensaba salirme de la escuela. Ya como no hablo mucho ingles y no entiendo mucho. Todavía no lo hablo muy bien y por seso yo pensaba salirme de la escuela. Pero ya que fui a verlo a usted hablar...cambie mes pensamientos y ahora boy a cavar la escuela y empezar una carrera. No lo digo adiós, sino hasta pronto.*

*Alex, Freshman in High School*

13. I learned a lot from you and you helped me to realize that I am a very special person. I learned that if it is to be it is up to me and that my heritage makes me special. You also helped my friends in my class to improve their confidence. How you used the words made it easy to understand my backpack.

Pierce, Fourth Grader

14. *Your presentation really opened my eyes to reality. You taught me to ignore others when they make smart or rude comments. You taught me that attitude really matters. To accept others, and to not treat others bad. My self esteem is high but you brought it even higher. You showed me to choose my friends carefully. You showed me to not compare myself to others for I am special and unique and I can be very successful.*

*Lauren, Seventh Grader*

191

15. *I cannot tell you how much I admire you. I must tell you that I came close to not coming to hear your program. Giving up a Saturday morning — it was my birthday — and like any teenager I hesitated when my friends asked me to go with them to this meeting. However, for some reason I decided to go anyway. Let me tell you that I am very glad I made the decision to go. Listening to you speak was the perfect birthday present I could have received. Your words inspired me so much and I had a great time. I have always been a very optimistic person with positive goals. I feel you have made me feel that I can even go further and do more with my positive attitude. You are right when you said that we will never see a 'backpack' the same way.*

*Virginia, Junior in High School*

16. I want to thank you for the way you have motivated me to go on with my life. I can honestly say that you have really changed my life. Jimmy, before I heard your presentation I felt the way you did when you were 9 years old. Maybe for different reasons but it all amounts to the same feelings: "Why live?" I will not bore you with my problems but I just wish that every person in the world could listen to you the way we were honored. I now have every reason in the world to live and I will make the best of my life. I also want to tell you that I've released the BUGS!!! And if everyone could do the same the world would be a lot different and better. You inspired me to keep on going, never to give up, and to ALWAYS keep my head up. I promise you that I will always try harder and walk with confidence.

Claudia, Senior in High School

17. Thank you very much for the motivational speech you gave here, I found it interesting and helpful. I appreciate this even more, because I thought that we were going to attend some boring speech. Not only did I like your speech, but I have also found myself applying the ideas you shared with us in my daily life. You have a very good way with words and know how to express yourself without misunderstanding and monotony. The problem, I think, with today's youth is that they are not well informed of the possibilities they have and the consequences of their bad actions. I say this because if more youth could hear your presentations it would help them to become more successful and make the right decisions.

Iesha, Senior in High School

18. I learned so many things from your backpack presentation. You made me see the world in a different view. I kind of knew of the things that were out there for me but I never bothered to do anything about it because I thought they were hard to accomplish. After listening to you I now realize that it's up to me, and that I have to put effort into what I want to do. Thank you Jimmy for making me realize that I can make a difference in school, at home, and in my community. I know that every thing I do in school will affect my future in a positive way. I am glad you made me see the positives of everything I can accomplish. I know that if it is to be it is up to me. I will never give up and always think positive.

Ivette, Junior in High School

19. First of all I want to thank you again for speaking to us. You really did motivate and made me think about many things. I am the kind of person who wouldn't pay attention to people who are "motivational speakers," but you were different. You not only motivated us, you made us think about what you were saying. I learned that in our backpack of life we must always have certain things if we want to succeed in life. Like always believing in myself, good attitude, and be committed to whatever it is I want to do. "People will pay you for what you know" is also something that stuck out in my mind, for I must put knowledge in my backpack. All I have to say is that you will be one of the people I will have to thank later on in my future for my success. You made me realize that some things that to me were not important, are the most important.

Wendy, Senior in High School

20. I enjoyed the speech you gave. I learned many tips and how to apply them on an every day basis. The most important tip I learned was to act on the belief I can. Next year I am going to the Technical Institute and you made me realize that I am under construction and looking for direction. I liked your concept of the good seed and bad seed. I will get rid of the bugs. Another thing I learned was to have high expectations when working with others. Trust and respect yourself and others. I am not going to allow others to distract me from reaching my goals, therefore, like you said to turn the negative into positives. Turn disadvantages into advantages, turning adversities into lessons. Instead of asking why? Start asking what I can learn from this. Like you suggested I walked out of your workshop MAD, I plan to Make A Difference. I will survive the plom disease and become successful and never give up my goals and dreams.

Miguel, Senior in High School

194

21. I am a 12 year old student at this middle school. I have bipolar disorder, otherwise known as depression. I'm having serious problems right now, and have been for a long time. I have been hospitalized before and I was afraid I might be again. But, with the help of my mother, and your program, I have learned that there are people with the same problems, and there is always tomorrow. I will always think about what I learned from your presentation, and I will never, never, never, never give up hope.

NS, Sixth Grader

22. You recently visited my school and I am writing you this letter to show my appreciation for giving me and my friends the inspiration we need to succeed. I believe that you have motivated us all to follow our dreams and to build a better future. I know that many of us would not have even considered the thought of going to college, but you have changed our perspectives on college. You have given us the reality of what going to college may offer us. I feel your words have given us all a little strength to continue our education and to finish it by going to college. Furthermore, you have also shown me that your attitude is a really important attribute in life. Your attitude not only reflects what kind of person you are but it reflects what kind of a person you will become. Your attitude determines your future. Also, I have learned that you should be proud of your heritage and your nationality. This is very useful, living in a nation where there are so many races, religions and nationalities. Mr. Jimmy, you have changed many lives so far. I know you are one of the greatest motivational speakers that have come to our school.

Liz, Seventh Grader

23. *I have always disliked pep rallies, assembles, motivational speeches, etc., but I truly enjoyed your speech. You used techniques that are not only easy to remember, but fun to say. You really captured my attention with the idea of the "backpack." I think that it is an outstanding way to say that everything you do influences your life. I have never experienced a speech that was so interactive, either. I liked the way you incorporated the students into your speech. I learned that no matter what happens to you, it will always depend upon your attitude. As you said, "Attitude is everything." I learned that you have to be confident in yourself. You didn't drone on and on about drugs, smoking, or drinking, but the stories you did tell made sense, especially the story about your daughter. It made sense and encouraged me to always tell the truth about everything. Your presentation has already helped me become a better student in only three days. Please come back next year to talk to more students.*

*J.J., Seventh Grader*

24. I appreciate you coming to our school. While you were talking to us I felt my self-esteem go higher and higher. I learned a lot about what you had to say to us, and I think everybody else did too. I have learned if it is to be it is up to me and everybody should be saying that when they get up in the morning. I learned the meaning of B.A.C.K.P.A.C.K. If everybody did what each letter stood for, society would be safer and incredibly nicer than what society is now. You are one cool person and we will not forget to put the right things in our backpacks.

Roger, Eighth Grader

25. I just wanted to thank you again for your wonderful presentation. After our meeting was over, I received one of your posters. When I got home, I hung it on the back of my door, so that before I leave my room, I take a glance at it, and check myself. I want to make sure that my backpack is ready for the day. I remember the exact words you said…if it is to be it is up to me. I strongly believe in this statement. I remember everything you said about my backpack and if I forget, I can just look at the backpack poster on my door.

My backpack is full…right about now!

> Believe in yourself
>
> Attitude is everything
>
> Courage is essential
>
> Knowledge (applied) is power
>
> People skills build respect
>
> Always set goals
>
> Commitment pays off
>
> Keep on dreaming

Thank you again Mr. Cabrera! I wish that we could have more speakers like you who actually reach us, and talk to us on our level. Some grown ups (not to be rude) come in here and talk down to us, like every thing they say is right, and that everything we do is wrong! I do respect others, so I really don't say anything. Anyway, I just wanted to thank you and write you this letter like I promised I would. It is because of your inspiring words that I will continue to be proud of who I am, and never give up.

Angela, Senior in High School

26. *I really enjoyed your presentation. I learned a great formula for success: Passion leads to Desire which leads to Work which leads to Success. I also came to realize that I was one of those people who walked in here with an "I can't" attitude. I learned that what I was really saying was that I won't. Now I believe in myself and have learned that through adversity comes abundance and that I need to control what I let absorb in my mind, and that the type of people I hang out with have a reflection of me. I really appreciate your coming today, your words have sank deep. In my mind and to me that is knowledge that I will never forget.*

*Ashley, Senior in High School*

27. I learned to treat people the way that I want to be treated...I learned that I'm not better than anyone else in this world. We are all the same and should respect each other. I learned why it's important to respect the other people who are around me. I got to see the life of someone else. I saw how hard your life was compared to mine. You showed us that you weren't just a boring teacher, but a teacher who wants to have fun as much as we do. You showed us that you were actually a kid at some point in time. You really made us listen to you. Everything that you said we know was probably going to happen sometime, somewhere, somehow. You showed everybody in there that we were just as good as everyone else. Thank you for showing us how to grow up, be successful, and most of all be happy for who we are, not who we look like, but who we really are.

Kenny, Seventh Grader

28. In your assembly I learned a lot of things. I learned that you should treat others the way you want to be treated, and I still remember the five fingers, if it is to be it is up to me. Don't worry Mr. Jimmy I won't forget these words. Thank you for talking to us about the Terra Nova and how to do our best on that test. I learned not to hate our lives just because we can't do what we want. You also taught me that we should share things with people and we should be careful about who we hang out with. You've been such a good inspiration to me and all of us kids. You remind me of my grandpa because you are nice, funny and cool. I learned a lot from him and now I have learned a lot from you.

T.R., Sixth Grader

29. I want to thank you for coming to our school to help us prepare for the TAAS. The way you explained TAAS was cool. Like each letter stood for something. The T for total you, A for attitude is everything, A for all about me and my future, S for my success. The way you did it was intuitive and motivating. It opened my eyes and mind to many new ideas. I explored all sorts of different brainstorming methods. You told us why we should believe in ourselves, have high self esteem, and be proud of our heritage. I really liked the part of getting rid of the BUGS. How to avoid the PLOM disease and be successful.

Thomas, Sophomore in High School

30. I am a sophomore and I've just recently taken the TAAS test. I felt very prepared because of a motivational speaker, Mr. Jimmy Cabrera. Mr. Jimmy really inspired me to keep on going. He talked about believing in myself, never to stop dreaming, and that attitude is everything. Then when I was taking the TAAS I really believed in myself and I was totally mentally prepared. I knew I was prepared for the TAAS. I told my parents about Mr. Jimmy and they were glad that I was better prepared for the TAAS. I have never been as motivated by anyone. I know for sure now I want to become a doctor. Thank you.

Sonia, Sophomore in High School

31. How have you been doing? I am doing fine and I remember some things from your speech. I like the idea about good seeds and bad seeds. Well, ever since that speech you made, I've been staying out of trouble and my grades have gone to 80 and above. You are the first person that has made me think. My parents have, but the way you showed us made the difference. You really made me think and I am glad. Because a few weeks before, I had been talking to a gang member. He was going to jail for criminal mischief and capital murder. I was good friends with him but I stopped talking to him because of what you said to us. I know if I continued to talk with him and hang out with him I could become like him. I am gonna keep improving my behavior. Please write back.

Carlos, Junior in High School

32. I learned from your speech to never be ashamed of yourself. Even if you don't know English. When I came to America I was 3 years old and could not speak or write English. Everyone laughed at me. But you reminded me how proud I am of myself. I also learned from you to never give up. Even if you don't know how to do it. Try and try. Don't give up.

Andres, Fifth Grader

33. Thank you for coming all the way from Texas to talk to us. I also want to thank you for giving us all of the good information. I learned a lot of things that I will never forget that will always be in my backpack. I will never forget that one person can make a difference and change the world. Each letter in backpack had a great meaning and you showed us I CAN with AmerICAN and MexICAN. I will never forget to leave the BUGS. I was inspired by applied knowledge is power and not just knowledge. Your information will not go to waste because I will use it in my life.

Jose, Seventh Grader

34. *I can't say thank you enough for coming to our school. First of all I was really nervous about the T.A.A.S., and I really didn't know what to do besides telling myself to be calm in every way I can. But there was just something there about overcoming my fear and that was the word — CONFIDENCE. Jimmy you taught that we need confidence in ourselves, but some of us didn't believe we did. I was one of them. You really helped me to be better prepared and after hearing your presentation I want you know that I had great confidence. Your ideas really helped me in many ways and now I am better prepared to face tomorrow.*

*Angela, Sophomore in High School*

35. I really enjoyed your speech and I can say that I am sure that you reached many kids here at this school. You came into my life, today, and you have given me more determination, support, and motivation than what my parents have given me. I'm not saying they are mean but they don't know how to support me. They sometimes don't even look at my report card. You helped me to keep thinking about my goal to go into the medical profession. I will tell my parents about your speech and maybe they will see how much I need their support. I wrote a little poem after hearing your speech. I hope you like it.

### Say No to Drugs

Someday you'll learn
About saying no,
You'll be proud of yourself for doing so.

No one is making you
On this I guarantee;

Tomorrow is a new day
On the corner of the street.

Don't turn your back on this new day,
Recall the scenes
Under which your friends have been, so
Grab a hold of yourself and
SAY NO TO DRUGS

Rosa, Sophomore in High School

# Index

# About the Author

Jimmy Cabrera is a dynamic and energetic speaker, riveting his audience's attention with his unique blend of motivation and education. Since 1983, over one million people from the corporate and educational communities have experienced his high-energy presentations. Jimmy has earned the National Speakers Association Certified Speaking Professional (CSP) designation – a distinction earned by less than 8% of the approximately 4,000 members within this association.

Jimmy is ranked by the research firm, Market Data Enterprises, as one of the top three Hispanic Motivational Speakers in the nation. (Hispanic Business Magazine, April 2002)

As a leader, Jimmy's philosophy is, "Don't count what you have, but what you have given – that total equals your success." Jimmy learned some tough lessons early in his life. As a Hispanic, he was reared in a predominately segregated community. Except for his parents, he had the feeling that no one cared. He experienced bitter rejection and prejudice from a society that labeled him "different." Eventually he realized that though you cannot forget the past and the pain, you can forgive and turn the negatives into POSITIVE learning experiences to ensure success.

Jimmy has the unique ability to guide youth, as well as adults, in the quest for success. His clients are assured success because Jimmy cares and makes certain that they use their utmost hidden potential. He helps his clients in the areas of Leadership, Mastering Change, Motivation, Diversity, Extraordinary Customer Service, Peak Performance, Sales and Team Building. His prestigious client list includes: United Way of America, SBC, Department of Interior, United States Hispanic Leadership Institute and Walt Disney World, as well as over 700 schools, colleges and churches.

---

To inquire about scheduling Jimmy Cabrera to speak  or to request additional information or books, contact:

## Success Through Excellence, Inc.
1827 Roanwood Drive • Houston, TX 77090-2026
(800)437-4226 • (281)537-0032 • fax (281)537-9242

e-mail: Hola100@JimmySpeaks.com
website: www.JimmySpeaks.com